Controlling the Difficult Adolescent:
The REST Program

(The Real Economy System for Teens)

David B. Stein, Ph.d.

UNIVERSITY
PRESS OF
AMERICA

Lanham • New York • London

Copyright © 1990 by
University Press of America®, Inc.
4720 Boston Way
Lanham, Maryland 20706

3 Henrietta Street
London WC2E 8LU England

Library of Congress Cataloging-in-Publication Data

Stein, David B.
Controlling the difficult adolescent : the REST program
(the real economy system for teens) / by David B. Stein.
p.   cm.
Includes bibliographical references.
1. Conduct disorders in adolescence—Popular works.
2. Problem youth—Rehabilitation.   I. Title.
RJ506.C65S74   1990   616.89'022—dc20   90–33888 CIP

ISBN 0–8191–7829-2 (alk. paper)
ISBN 0-8191-7830-6 (pbk. : alk. paper)

Dedication

To my wonderful children
Heidi, Alex, and Kevin
With Love,
Dad

Table of Contents

Preface

Over ten years ago, while I was a fulltime private practitioner, I became aware of my inadequacy as a therapist with adolescents. Sessions with many teenagers were typically monosyllabic exchanges, shoulder shrugs, and general noncooperation. Out of a strong sense of frustration, I thought that in order to overcome my apparent shortcomings some time in the library delving into the adolescent treatment literature would be the logical thing to do. I soon realized that a something was missing in the literature. Nothing clearly seemed to help with these cases. I inquired of my colleagues. They too expressed frustration and had little to offer about how to proceed. Many of the colleagues stated that the obvious course of action was to commit these teenagers to psychiatric hospitals for "treatment."

Further inquiry into this so called hospital based treatment led to the conclusion that the usual grab bag of group therapy, individual therapy and even chemo-therapy were no more effective than the outpatient methods. I found that the children were rotated from hospital to hospital with little apparent improvement.

Several years later when I had returned to academia, I developed a questionnaire as a research project that was sent to two hundred and fifty psychiatric hospitals offering treatment services to adolescents. The questionnaire specifically asked what treatment methods were used, what progress occurred, what were the grounds for terminating cases, were there any follow-up studies, etc., etc. Not one single hospital returned the questionnaire.

Eventually, I concluded that the freedom of children was forceably being taken from them under the guise of "treatment" when in fact no such effective treatment methods existed. This condition still exists. I suspect that this issue is a time bomb that shortly will explode in the face of mental health professionals in the form of either disgrace or litigation.

The methods offered in this book are intended to attack the problem of developing an effective system of outpatient treatment tools for difficult adolescents. The methods herein offered are not pretentiously assumed to be a panacea of adolescent therapy that will cure the existing problems. It is hoped that the methods help reduce the frustrations of therapists and give them some viable tools that they can grab hold of and thus reduce the need of locking children up. It is also hoped that what is offered in this book has heuristic value so that new ideas and new methods are developed to further reduce the severity of this problem.

I wrote this book in simple language addressing it to parents. It can be used as a manual by parents to deal with a difficult adolescent. The methods presented in this book are based on years of research which is now in part available in the professional literature. However, I am aware that professionals frequently use materials from the commercial market as part of their treatment packages and I hope that this book will lend utility and merit in their clinical work.

While the methods introduced are clearly behavioral they do not obviate the use of additional methods. These methods are intended to "put the brakes on" the difficult adolescent so that more traditional communicative and cognitive methods have a better chance of succeeding. The teen, once brought under control, appears to be much more receptive to listen and to engage in more meaningful dialogue with the therapist.

Many readers may become aware that these techniques are rather powerful. Indeed they do put considerable "power" in the hands of both the parents and the therapist. Some therapists may even scream "coercion." I can only submit that it has been many years since I have needed to hospitalize a teenager. Once a disquieted household has been brought under control and positive, assertive communications substituted for screaming, or even hitting, both teens and parents subsequently report feeling a lot happier. Any scientific tool can be misused and abused. It is hoped that the parents will use the tools outlined in this book with love and good judgment.

I wish to thank Ed Smith, formerly chair of my department and now Associate Vice President of the college, for his strong encouragement and support. Dr. Smith also gave invaluable assistance for the research. Don Stuart, Academic Vice President of the college, took time from his overwhelming schedule to edit the manuscript. Heidi Shifflitt, a former student and now a high school teacher, tirelessly typed and retyped the manuscript. Cathi West, our department secretary, helped greatly with the typing. Amy Alvis and Karen Raymond, two of the best students I've ever been privileged to supervise, helped greatly with the literature research.

Introduction

Controlling the
Difficult Adolescent

Contrary to myth, adolescence is often a time of joy. Parents may experience the wonder of seeing their children transform before their eyes. Few things can be more fulfilling than to see our youth confronting and overcoming social, educational, physical, and sexual difficulties.

Closeness between parent and child may evolve through open expression of thoughts and feelings. This is the period in life when attitudes and values are formed concerning the most difficult, explosive, and embarrassing topics. Parents must be prepared to listen to their children talk about drugs, sex, peer pressures, and careers. Only when there is a closeness, and a feeling of trust, will the youngsters turn to their parents for advice. As the youth and parent share, a wonderful bond of intimacy can develop.

Unfortunately, most parents reading a book such as this, and typically the parents I see at my office, want to immediately learn how to discipline and punish their teen. However, I wish to make clear at the outset that parents will not experience success in bringing a difficult child under control unless there is a genuine loving relationship. The techniques outlined in later chapters are useful tools that can be easily implemented, and can indeed produce results, but the aim of this book is to bring a difficult child sufficiently under control so that a closer and more loving parent-child relationship can develop. In reviewing my years of research and clinical work with adolescents I discovered an interesting, but not unexpected pattern. A few of the cases using the programs outlined in this book were failures in which I found parents that either had difficulty in expressing love, both verbally and physically, or parents that were so narcissistic that their own interests superseded giving time and attention to their children. In other words, at some level there was an element of neglect toward the child. Frequently, in cases such as these, the programs would show initial improvements in the youth's conduct and attitudes, and shortly these gains would trickle away; invariably, in these cases I would find parents that were more interested in watching television, in burying their nose in a book, or in repairing the outside of the house than in talking to, or spending time with their child. Getting the adolescent under control is only a small part of the battle. An even larger part is giving of yourself and developing a loving relationship.

While the reasons for a misbehaving adolescent are complex, much of the difficulty can be attributed to a society where family structure is crumbling and where youth and adults experience loneliness and a lack of support. Gone for the most part, is the extended kinship family of the 1950's, diminished is the nuclear family of the 1960's, and instead common is the single parent family, divorce, and serial relations. Parents then find themselves combatting the vacuum created in our children by these societal forces. The only means I know of for succeeding is to give of your time and of yourself.

I am only too painfully aware of how difficult it is today for the American family. Two parent families find that both spouses have to work just to make ends meet, many women want careers for personal fulfillment, and of course there is the single parent. These parents all work exhausting hours only to come home each day to the additional stresses of shopping, cooking, cleaning and household chores. Suggestions for dealing with some of these problems will be discussed later. The important issue is that under the weight of all of this pressure we cannot forget that our children "need" our personal time.

Actually, I often remind parents that spending fun time with our children is a wonderful way to take time out from all the stress and to rejuvenate ourselves. My little girl is not yet a teenager, but I do take time from a busy schedule to be with her, and I plan, and hope to continue spending special time with her throughout her youth and well into her adult life as well. I feel marvelous after having spent a day with her. Often we lunch at a restaurant and then perhaps go for a walk in the park. We have also gone fishing, picnicking, sightseeing in a museum, or any number of other fun and interesting activities. She also spends many similar days with her mom, who incidentally has a busy career as a dentist. We also work at having lots of family time, which is important to all of us. The time a father spends camping with his son, or taking his daughter to a father-daughter school dance, or the time a mother takes to have lunch with her son, or to just go for a long walk - and - talk with her daughter is most crucial in their children's emotional development. I am not talking about the daily routine where we spend parallel time, but I am talking more about the quality time which is spent in fun and sharing.

I have heard arguments by parents claiming all sorts of things such as: they do not have such extravagantly available free time, that their teenager is not interested in spending time with them, or that they have several children and cannot possibly do this with all of them. I am not suggesting parents do this every weekend, but I am saying that once in a while it is critical to be with your child and to let them get to know you as a thinking, feeling person, and not just as an authority figure. You will have far fewer problems with your teenager when you have a close and loving relationship. I have heard too many parents say they do not have the time only to find that after a divorce the parent who does not have custody is suddenly free every weekend and on one weekday evening for being with their youngster. As for the teenager's attitude, well maybe they do want to spend most of their time with peers, but an occasional day with mom or dad is strongly desired by most teenagers.

In addition to taking actions that show your love it is also important that you say it. Do not assume a child knows what you are thinking. Words and actions are equally important.

Words of love may be conditional or unconditional. Conditional approval means praising a youngster for an accomplishment or for any effort. Statements such as these help motivate and shape attitudes and behaviors. Sometimes I hear parents express the fear that if they constantly reinforce their child then "won't they become an approval seeker?" It seems just the opposite occurs, that is youngsters abundantly praised grow up secure. The approval seeker often comes from a cold, stern, and critical home, where a word of praise is a rare or nonexistent event. Words of love may also be unconditional, such as a simple "I love you," where the child does not have to perform to earn your approval. In either case, saying it is what is crucial to your relationship and also to your child's emerging self-image and self-esteem.

While expressions of love are critical, the key to overall success is structure. The formula outlined in this book is a combination of firm structure and love. Parents have been made to fear that by being firm their child will be psychologically scarred, or they will lose their child's love. Historically, psychologists and psychiatrists have probably contributed considerably to these silly fears. Neither is true. How or in what manner you are firm is the important issue. Being firm in an aggressive manner, that is by yelling, screaming, and hitting will indeed engender resentment in your child, will badly damage your relationship, and as we will see later, in the chapter on punishment, it does not work. Not being firm at all will only lead to your losing your child's respect, and again will injure your relationship. Being firm in an assertive way, and applying consistent and meaningful consequences will be the central theme of the techniques outlined in this book.

Chapter 1

How Did It Happen?

When a child manifests marked behavioral problems and displays attitudes of mindless, insensitive stupidity, parents are often overcome with self-blame and guilt, believing; "I created the monster!". The reality is that most parents I have met deeply love their children, and worry endlessly whether what they are doing is correct and whether their children will turn out O.K. But, that still does not answer the burdening question of how - how did it go wrong?

There are no clear or simple answers. As mentioned previously, the breakdown of the family unit has contributed considerably. The loss of basic familial systems of love and support is leading our children to growing up in a society of intense loneliness and alienation. Misbehavior can often be an expression of a child's anger when growing up with unsatisfied needs for affiliation. Sadness and anger often go hand in hand and occur when we feel alone and lonely. This is a heavy burden for a child to carry.

We must also consider the decay of religious and moral values. Parents are confused about what to teach their children, so they often either avoid teaching or communicating a solid set of beliefs and values. The attitudes of the adolescent wind up being an expression of confusion of what is right or wrong and what is appropriate or not appropriate. Today if parents are going to teach children values then the parents must consciously explore and decide their own values. The young adults in the 1960's began rejecting traditional thought and practice. Unfortunately it has proved much more difficult to replace these values in a meaningful and sensible way. Children in succeeding generations appear to reflect the loss of these basic values by expressing more and more undisciplined manners and behaviors.

Oddly, the contradictory conditions of poverty and affluence can underlie difficulties with the teenage sub-culture. How poverty contributes to the problems of adolescents has been written about extensively. The effects of poor living conditions are beyond the scope of

5

this text, since solutions entail broad and sweeping strides for society to eliminate poverty itself. At the other extreme affluence has contributed to the evolving problems we are currently experiencing with teens. The effects of affluence are subtle and even more difficult to understand. All too often I witness a family where the parents sacrificed and worked hard to climb the mobility ladder and try to afford for their children the finest opportunities and the best material advantages only to see their young drop out of school, or assume jobs several steps back down the socio-economic scale. Parents often complain why their young cannot see the light, and they ask, "Why don't the kids have the stuff to make it in life?" Why are the teenagers more interested in hanging around and having fun than in taking school seriously and fighting hard for a good, solid career? Why are they more interested in sassing and being rude than in listening to all the brilliant advice we have for them? Well why not? We have set the conditions for mindlessness. We have set the stage so that goal setting, sacrifice, forethought, planning, and achieving are not necessary. All a youngster has to do is just put their two feet on a plushly carpeted bedroom floor each morning and miraculously they are surrounded by stereos, T.V.'s, clock radios, telephones, cars, motorcycles, good food, a beautifully well furnished house, etc., etc. It took me a long time to realize that many teenagers sitting opposite me in my office had little else going on between the right and left ears than Rock FM 104. Is it possible that in what we have striven so hard for, to give our children the best, we may indeed have been in error when we have given them too much too easily. The guidelines of this book will deal with requiring more from our young and expecting responsible and thoughtful behavior in earning all those wonderful material comforts.

Mindlessness in a teenager can also be the product of over zealous or overly strict parenting during the infant and pre-adolescent years. Parents often say "He was such a good boy, why did he suddenly change?" It is quite easy to mistake the compliant child for the good child. When the parent is over controlling they are preventing the child from experiencing consequences which help the child to learn decision making and problem solving skills. When the compliant child turns thirteen they may challenge the dominance of the family hierarchy, and if their cognitive skills are insufficiently developed the home may be terrorized by a thoughtless bullying creature. The same condition can also produce a child that is lazy and clumsy. This is a kid that cannot seem to do anything right, when the reality is that they indeed are children who do not seem to think because they have been trained not to think.

In parenting, the extreme opposite of an overly controlling family is the overly liberal family. Under such family conditions the child insufficiently internalizes a sense of right and wrong. Their behaviors can be a reflection of a poorly developed conscience, where their acts are not only insensitive to the rights and feelings of others, but may also defeat purposeful and meaningful goal directed accomplishments for the teenagers themselves. It is time for parents to stop being afraid to parent. Allowing a youngster too much freedom can handicap them throughout life because they will be unable to impose the limits necessary to live in civilized society. If a child is going to live successfully they must be taught rules and guidelines. This entails not only a responsibility for the parent to teach proper values, but most importantly to serve as exemplary models. There is no getting away from it, modelling is the most powreful way to teach our children. What they become later in life will largely be the result of what they observe in us. If they see us sit night after night hypnotized in front of the T.V., then there is a good chance they will develop lazy minds. If they see us drink excessively, it is likely they will wind up doing the same. If they see us take drugs indiscriminately, whether prescription or otherwise, what is it to prevent them from doing the same? If they see us readily yell, scream and hit, then it is likely they will learn to respond to frustration with aggression. Remember this - what we say to our children is far weaker in their learning process than what they see us doing. Before we start being critical of them, let us examine ourselves. Therefore, firm parenting not only involves the learning of techniques for implementing firmness, but also the responsibility of exemplifying what we are asking of our children.

I do not wish to excuse adolescent misbehaviors. However, it is important to take into consideration pressures they are going through that may be contributing to their misbehaviors. The hallmark of puberty is, of course, the bodily changes experienced by the youngster. Hormonal changes, growth spurts, and the emergence of secondary sex characteristics may exacerbate mood swings in the young. They often report a vague sense of malaise, a sort of edgy feeling they cannot explain. During such times their stress tolerance level may ebb and social circumstances add to their stress load. School work dramatically becomes more difficult and demanding. Peer pressures can tear at loyalties with parents. There are increases in sexual urges. Dating brings the ever present threat of rejection. Conformity in dress codes and behaviors add still more pressure. The pressure to fit in may include the push to experiment with drugs and alcohol. The desire for social acceptance is particularly heightened at this time.

7

This combination of biological and social stresses makes it difficult for the adolescent to cope. When the pressures are overwhelming to the youngster they may take out their frustrations where it is perceived safest to do so, mainly in the home and usually directed at the parents. When asked what is bothering them, the adolescent may not be able to identify what all these strange feelings are. In addition, they probably do not have the insight skills to cut through the myriad of stresses to identify what is the problem. In any event they may direct these uneasy feelings toward their parents in a variety of ways. Their tone of voice may become sarcastic and they may shoot hate stares and eye rolls as if to say, "You're so dumb, how did you ever make it to middle age?". They may withdraw to their room for many hours and hide from their hurts by practically hypnotizing themselves with stereo music. Flare ups in the form of temper tantrums, usually over very minor events, may become commonplace. Parental attempts at communication may be thwarted with demands to "Get off my case!". When an adolescent is out of control this way, talking to them, whether directed from the parent or from a therapist, does little good. Often the youngster has set up such a strong barrier of defensiveness that, if left unchecked, neither the parent nor the therapist will be able to break through. Under such circumstances only forcing the teenager to regain control will open the lines of communication and then the youth may be receptive to reason. Sometimes a direct talk therapy, cognitive-reasoning approach does work with adolescents and in those instances therapy is a piece of cake. However, for the highly resistant youngster, it is only by having them put the brakes on that the therapist or parents will begin to get through to them. In some instances to reach this point a very tough stance may have to be assumed, and that does not mean the use of physical devices in the form of screaming and hitting because this only heightens the youth's resistance and makes matters worse. Alternative and more productive techniques will be offered. Interestingly, once the child is brought under control I have not only observed a more reasonable person but a youngster that seems more at peace, as if saying thank you for the structure. It is then that the communications and relationships between parent and child can be worked on.

Where reason does not prevail with the normal but difficult adolescent, matters become enormously more complicated when drugs/alcohol are involved. This is not an invitation to over-react if the parents discover their teenager has tried drugs and/or alcohol; almost all teenagers will at some point experiment with chemicals and probably most of them will occasionally consume something during their social activities. I personally feel that this widespread availability and use of chemicals is a national disgrace. However, the main danger for the occasional user is driving while intoxicated. When a parent is faced with a youngster regularly using chemicals indicating a strong possibility of psychological and perhaps even physical dependency, then matters are indeed critical. The power chemicals can have over a youngster's behavior and emotions is frightening. When this occurs very strong measures may have to be taken jointly by parents and the therapist. Recent innovative techniques have begun to prove useful in dealing with adolescents with chemical dependencies. These methods will be outlined for the parents in the chapter "What is Toughlove".

Acting out misbehaviors of the adolescent may be the product of their school experiences. Recently, considerable media attention has been paid to the weakness of quality in our nation's school systems. I applaud the attention and efforts to improve the quality of education in this country, but there is an additional issue that also needs to be addressed. The needs of many teenagers are not being met. Many high schools gear their curriculum to students as if they were all heading to the finest universities and colleges. Practical needs and considerations are ignored; the result of this is the integration of college bound and non-college bound students. The non-college bound student is bored and turned off to material they consider uninteresting, irrelevant to their life goals, abstract, and way above their heads. They end up failing such courses. What follows is a downward spiral in self-esteem, and a barrage of parental accusations, finger pointing, and frustrations. No wonder such youngsters may act out in anger, misbehaving, or simply turning off with indifference. The logic eludes me why school systems have dropped track programs that specialize in hands-on training emphasizing vocational career skills and integrating abstract with vocational courses. Integrating such lost youngsters in courses with college bound teenagers also results in the watering down of quality levels of the preparatory courses. Thus, the college oriented student is cheated of his or her courses being the strongest possible preparation for their goals. To upgrade the quality of courses benefits the college bound student, but increases the frustrations and sense of failure of the non-college bound student, i. e. Catch 22. This country still reflects its history of elitism in education, for a "cultured gentleman". Many youngsters graduate from high school, if they even make it that far, to find out they have been sold a bill of goods - that they are supposed to be prepared for adult life and the job market, when in fact they are prepared for neither. Then they must either return to school for additional, and often expensive, specialty training, or survive on minimum

9

wages as unskilled laborers.

County school systems may provide a token vocational school, but often they are inadequate and end up filled before meeting the needs of vast numbers of other youngsters. Transportation is often poorly provided and inaccessible to many. Plus, such schools are often given second class citizenship and therefore, many youngsters are reluctant to apply to these programs for fear of being labeled as dumb. Wouldn't our children's needs best be met by providing alternatives within all schools? The only way schools will sufficiently provide the quality and success to meet the needs of our young is if parents become involved. Our schools will improve when the PTA's are not just a forum for cake sales, but are a medium for overseeing the activities of each school. Parents should not only demand the best quality in education but some good common sense as to the services provided our children - let us not forget we are footing the bill, and we have a right to our money's worth. I believe the number of problem cases will decrease when schools are providing more programs suited for non-college bound teens.

When reviewing the causes for difficult adolescent behaviors, we cannot neglect an additional but important issue - parental overreaction. The young will be young! They are going to be mischievous at times, they will experiment, they will test the lines of authority, and they do become confused and sometimes justifiably upset. I strongly urge parental authority over teenagers, but lattitude for normal adolescent insanity should be allowed. Oddly, if most of us were to have been punished for what we did as teens we still would be serving sentences in Sing Sing, yet when we reflect on our misdeeds we sometimes smile and secretly wish we had the nerve to do it all over again.

This is not to give a license for disrespect or for behaviors that are going to endanger life and limb. We certainly should not allow for angry, irresponsible, and abusive behaviors in the home, or for permitting a child to continue on a road of self destruction. However, occasional foolishness and comic mischievousness is often harmless and is not deserving of explosive parental rage.

I will be introducing methods for controlling adolescent behaviors, but I hope, parents will not abuse these techniques and use them to over-control a youngster. These methods are simply tools and their application and use should be administered with good judgment and common sense. This should not be a means for excessively controlling a child's every breath, but a way of making peace and opening the door for love and communication.

One final word. Parents often say they will just wait out these

10

rough years and eventually the adolescent will grow up. There is much validity in such a statement, but it is not just a product of chronological growth. When a youngster approaches eighteen the realities of life begin to encroach on their awareness. The consequences of mindless non-productivity begin to become painfully apparent. The parents begin to withdraw much of the protective sugar coating and the adolescent fears moving out into the great big world. The emergence of the contingencies of real life then begin to modify the youngster's thinking and behavior. The adolescent then begins thinking, evaluating, and planning responsible behavior in order to survive. Often, for the first time the adolescent begins to assess jobs, potential income, and what it takes financially to maintain a given lifestyle. In other words, they finally begin to think. This is not always the case because going to college or continuing to live at home can prolong the adolescent mentality. Since I began teaching in college I realized the illusions of independence such an atmosphere perpetuates. It is really quite a protective environment, where almost every aspect of the youth's life has been planned. Social intercourse and activities are more readily provided than at any other time in life. Laundry and meals are provided. Almost all expenses are met by checks from home. Eventually, though, this too will end and the youngster will have to face adult life and responsibilities. I must admit enviably what a great time college life can be.

Whether at the end of college or high school, it is the changing mentality of the parents that allows the youth to grow up. As the protective umbrella is removed the youngster begins to mobilize for survival. It is then that they begin to grow up. Sometimes parents extend their protectiveness well beyond what is healthy. They allow a child who is unable to make a living, or a child who spends his money on drugs, or a dependent child to perpetuate his helplessness by staying at home. Out of a distorted sense of guilt, the parents continue to provide a secure and protected home environment, even when the youngster is abusive. I have seen this continue to the age of 30 and even higher. Such overprotectiveness interferes with healthy emotional and psychological development. It serves as an injustice to the young. Once we have taught them to fly, we must push them out of the nest.

11

Chapter 2

Discipline and Punishment

Before introducing the techniques for controlling adolescent behaviors I feel it is wise to review why the method presented in this text evolved. To do this it is important to understand why traditional parenting methods of punishment frequently fail.

We tend to worship punishment. Whenever I teach a course in early childhood parenting the parents cannot wait to get to the how-to-punish part. I learned over the years that to keep their attention I would leave the topic of punishment for last. I do this not to prolong the course, but to be certain the parents actively attend the more important topics of reinforcement. Positive social reinforcement in the form of expressions of praise and love are far more powerful, in the mental, emotional, and behavioral development of a child, than punishment. Just reflect for a moment on your observations of parenting in your friends, your family, and even yourselves. Little Johnny sits quietly playing or watching T.V. peacefully for hours - and does anyone go over to him to praise him, or hug and kiss him for being so well behaved? But let him say boo in the wrong way and then the yelling, screaming, threats and even the occasional whack emerge.

If your primary method of raising children is negative then why be surprised if they turn on us when they begin testing their power in the early teens. Predominant use of punishment does not build relationships; it may control behaviors but it does nothing to build closeness.

Our preference to punish or use negative responses in attempting to control the behaviors of others is pervasive. Even in marriage, as the years go by, most couples become increasingly negative toward each other. During courtship we try to look good for each other by dressing carefully, we listen to each other attentively, we praise each other constructively and we sit close and snuggly. But as the years go by we tend to criticize, we ignore, and we argue - the compliments stop and expressions of love become rare. Many of us are heard to say that we can tell how long a couple has been married by how far they sit apart in the car. Even my daughter has commented inquisitively about seeing couples in restaurants who sit through an entire meal hardly saying a word to each other.

In the classroom children have to sit through years of regimentation and hard work rarely hearing a word of praise or encouragement. During any given academic day in a class of thirty children approximately three to five of them will be reinforced by their teacher and the rest will be ignored, criticized, or yelled at. The ones that are reinforced are usually the better students, although the others probably need the praise even more. Is it a wonder that after ten or twelve years in such an environment youngsters can become turned off to education?

When, at work, was the last time you received a word, or a note, praising you for your long and hard hours of dedicated effort? Step out of line once and you will think the roof caved in. How much more pleasant working conditions would be and how much greater would company loyalty be, if we only heard a positive word of caring.

Punishment is obviously a major issue in human transactions. Therefore, it may help to understand its effectiveness, and its limitations.

What We Need to Know

Parents often complain of their children: "I yell at her, I scream at her, I hit her and no sooner turn around and she is doing it again! Doctor, is she insane? What is the matter with that child?"

In my practice insane children are rare, emotionally impaired children are rare, but misbehaving children are common. What parents are saying in this context is actually a frequent result of punishment. Punishment only acts as a temporary suppressor of behavior. This rule applies to both the behavior of children as well as adults. When the punishment stops the behavior returns. Perhaps not immediately, but it will return. In fact, punishment suppresses a misbehavior rather quickly, that is it gives a quick, instantaneous result. A major rule in psychology is that, "Immediate reinforcement is more powerful than delayed reinforcement." Therefore, when we apply punishment to our children we see immediate results which is actually reinforcing for us. By yelling "keep quiet", and experiencing a child immediately becoming quiet, we tend to become trained to rely on yelling. The fact that in the long run the behaviors we punish keep coming back does not seem to deter us from doing what we know has repeatedly given us immediate results. Therefore, we develop the habit of punishing, but the

14

children do not change. By developing the habit of punishment it eventually feels "normal" or comfortable to us, conversely by not practicing the habit of reinforcement it does not feel subjectively "normal", or comfortable to us. Reinforcement, even though more powerful in changing behavior, works slowly and therefore we do not experience the immediate and quick gratification of changed behavior. Because it works slowly it does not as readily become a habit for us and does not feel quite as comfortable. Thus, punishment is a suppressing tool. It does not teach new behaviors, but merely holds down behaviors; remove it and up pops the behavior again, and again. On the other hand, reinforcement does teach new behaviors. It is reinforcement that is a motivating and shaping tool for children to learn and improve behaviors.

The most effective way of working with children is to combine effective methods of punishment with active reinforcement. The punishment holds the inappropriate behaviors down, giving the parents the opportunity to use reinforcement to teach and shape new, more appropriate behaviors. However, this formula will work best if the punishment is of the correct type, the guidelines for which we will be discussing shortly.

It is possible that consistently applying severe punishment can lead to the permanent suppression of a behavior. However, the severe and consistent application of punishment can lead a child to becoming nervous, tense, fearful, and anxious. An anxiety ridden child does not learn well, and therefore, the learning of newer more appropriate responses will be blocked. Also, the tense child makes more mistakes, which in time leads to more parental frustration, anger, and even more punishment. Anxiety is one of the corner stones of neurotic behaviors. There is high likelihood that a child growing up in a punitive environment and becoming tense will develop neurotic coping patterns later in the teenage years or in adult life. Thus, the drawbacks of severe and consistent punishment far outweigh the possibility of any benefits; a specific behavior may indeed be suppressed at the expense of having an anxiety ridden child.

If the parent is using physical methods of punishment in the form of yelling, screaming, and hitting then it is important that they recognize that they are modeling how to handle frustrations. This means that when many parents become frustrated with their children's behaviors they respond with aggression. Modeling is the most powerful way of teaching our children, and if we are modeling aggression then we should expect our child to become aggressive. On many occasions I have witnessed parents either spanking their child or hitting them

15

across the face while saying, "Where have you learned such behavior, we teach you better than that at home." Again, there is a higher likelihood that in a child's emotional and behavioral development "what we model will supersede what we say." Aggressive children most frequently come from aggressive families.

The modeling of aggression does not have to be directed toward the child for it to be learned. It can be directed toward other children, between spouses, or even directed at inanimate objects. An occasional temper flare-up is normal, and parents need not feel guilty for occasionally succumbing to stress. However, frequent aggressiveness does indeed set the stage for what a child learns.

Children can adapt or habituate to extreme levels of physical pain. This adaption effect occurs when punishment is frequent; it is a survival response of the child. The adaption can be for tactile pain from hitting, or for auditory pain from yelling. Thus, over the years the parents would have to progressively increase the intensity of the hitting and yelling to get any results, and eventually a level will be reached where no results can be elicited. The child increasingly learns to tune out such a painful environment. Unfortunately, the anxieties will still be internalized. A child developing these reaction patterns will learn to keep everything inside, he very likely can become withdrawn and sullen. It may become too threatening for them to open up. Then their parents may wonder why the child will not communicate with them. A child that has effectively learned to tune out his environment may appear empty headed, obtuse, oblivious, and nonresponsive. They may in fact be missing many external environmental cues; by hiding in the safety of their private fantasy world, or even in shutting off their brain and hardly thinking at all. At any given time in my practice I will have an active case involving such a child. For therapy to begin to be successful I will have to involve the parents and work with them in understanding how detrimental their frequent fights are to the child, or what damage either parent is doing when in front of the child they explode, hitting the car, pounding walls, kicking chairs, or any other such silly but surprisingly frequent behaviors.

I am well aware that some therapists advocate such behaviors in adults as a means of ventilating pent-up emotions. When occasionally done in privacy maybe it is harmless, but in front of the child it can be frightening and confusing. Such ventilating of anger is often cited by therapists as being therapeutic and cleansing. Research however, shows that the overt expression of anger leads to more expressions of anger and gradually it becomes a habit. In the short run the individual may experience a temporary release of pressure, but in the long run they learn to continuously overreact to minor stresses and events prolonging their anger. Oddly, rather than solve the problems the overt expression of anger often excerbates the difficulty. A healthy alternative is assertive communications which not only effectively expresses one's feelings, but also encourages problem solving.

In technical language, punishment is supposed to be the application of an aversive stimulus that decreases the probability of a response. What if the application of the aversive stimulus was not only not decreasing the response, but actually maintaining or even increasing the response? Remember the sentence: "I yell at her, I scream at her and I turn around and she's doing it again! Is she insane?" What could actually be occurring when the parents believe they are punishing misbehaviors and yet the child is not only not improving but in fact getting worse. To understand better it is important to know the elements of social reinforcement:

    Paying attention,
    Spending time with,
    Talking to,
    Looking at,
    Listening to,
    Touching,
    and Just Plain Showing a Response.

Therefore, when a parent is yelling at, and hitting their child, they may actually be reinforcing the very behavior they wish to eliminate.

Just check each item:	Yes	No	Doubtful
-Is the parent paying attention	x		
-Are they spending time with the child	x		
-Are they talking to the child	x		
-Are they looking at the child	x		
-Are they listening to the child		x	
-Are they touching the child	x		
-Are they showing a response	You bet they are!		

This may not be reinforcement in the way the lay public might think of it, but to a professional observer of human behavior - any behavior that is being maintained or increased is being reinforced. The reinforcement just does not appear in the form we are used to, but from the child's perspective it is doing the job. To a child it is still a reinforcing form of attention, no matter how aversive and bewildering it may seem to the parent. As a matter of fact children will frequently misbehave just to receive these negative forms of attention. To a child the most

17

aversive condition is no attention at all, a complete absence of rein-forcement. Some therapy methods call this zero strokes; strokes ap-proximately mean some form of reinforcement. Ignoring a child is a form of zero strokes. It is analogous to a condition of sensory depriva-tion. As was stated earlier, this is a typical condition in most house-holds, where parents actually socially ignore their children when they are behaving well and abundantly give them attention, even if nega-tive, when misbehaving. Therefore, if a child is not being stroked pos-itively, and if they avoid the condition of zero strokes, where else can the child turn but to negative strokes, or negative forms of attention. When the child does this it may be in a vigorous and active manner, making the child appear like an annoying pain in the neck. Such a child is simply working at getting its stroking needs met.

What Are the General Characteristics of Effective Punishment

From the review of the research on punishment we can deduce that in many instances parents are not doing well in disciplining their chil-dren. They often feel a sense of frustration at being unable to control a difficult teenager; the overview is not intended to heighten parents' frustration, but to point out the importance of finding alternative and more effective methods of parenting. In this section we will review some general guidelines for effective discipline, and in the next chap-ter we will introduce specific methods for controlling the difficult teenager.

General Principle #1

For disciplining to be most effective it should be applied immedi-ately following the misbehavior. Ideally, the youngster should be pun-ished for a misbehavior when it is occurring. This improves the child's chances of associating the consequence with the actual act. When punishment is delayed, especially for a long period of time, its admin-istration may then occur when the child is behaving well, and conse-quently the child could develop the mental association of "What's the use of trying. I'm only going to get it anyway!" When the term "im-mediately" is used I am well aware that practical considerations must be made and that often it is quite inconvenient to punish in certain lo-cations, for example, in the midst of groups of people, or at Grandma and Grandpa's house. Therefore a good close approximation to immediate is "daily." This means the criteria for immediacy can be pragmatically met if the consequences are given on the day of misbehavior. If we think about the criterion for immediacy we can begin to see why one of the most traditional and frequently used methods of punishing teenagers, grounding, does not work. As a matter of fact as we review the other criteria we will see even further why grounding is not very effective. Roughly, grounding is the loss of one or several reinforcements or privileges for an intermediate period of time, usually one to six weeks. Often grounding is put into effect too late, such as on the day that report cards are distributed. It is not the receiving of the report card that should be punished, but the daily acts of poorly studying, and doing homework throughout the six week period. Then, the grounding remains in effect when the child has improved thus punishing the improved acts. That means if the child is grounded for six weeks and works hard to raise their grades they are still being punished during the period of increased effort. This can be very emotionally defeating. Usually, what happens next is the grounding is suspended when the next report card comes in and the grades nose dive again. The child has learned nothing and the parents are bewildered. If the child received effective consequences each day of the entire school year for doing sloppy homework, or for failing to study, then each day they have a new chance to get back on track and the chances are the parents would see considerably better results at the end of each six week report card period. In the next chapter we will review the specifics for doing this.

General Principle #2

The next principle is consistency. Punishment should not be sporadic or haphazard, which only confuses a child. "Inconsistency teaches persistency." This means that parents must decide which misbehaviors they wish to eliminate.

I have found parental inconsistency to be one of the most frequent problems when a misbehaving child is referred to my office for help. If the techniques outlined in this book are going to work then all parents must fully understand the importance of the principle of consistency. One of the Learning Disability tutors at the clinic asked me one day: "What are parents to do if they have considerable difficulty remaining consistent?" I suggested that such parents may have to participate in some personal therapeutic work before getting into working with their children. Fortunately, there are therapy techniques to assist patients in developing skills for more efficient functioning. In a nut shell, consistency is a top priority if parents wish to see improvement in the behaviors and attitudes of their teens.

General Principle #3

If punishment is to be applied with consistency then the next general rule is important - that the method of punishment should not produce tension or anxiety within the child. Therefore physical methods of punishment applied with any consistency would be ruled out since they are highly condusive to nervousness and tension.

I am often asked if I am against a good old fashioned spanking. Not necessarily - BUT - spanking should be reserved when all other "intelligent" methods have failed, and therefore should be used rarely. As a matter of fact for children under the age of twelve there are a wealth of highly effective discipline techniques that not only require no physical interaction but also do not make a child nervous. For children above the age of twelve I am against the use of any spanking; for a teenager a spanking can be an extremely degrading and humiliating experience. A spanking, a paddling, or a smack across the face can be very ego damaging. It would not only fail to control their behaviors but would engender extreme anger and resentment resulting in a distancing and in a breakdown of communications. So, for the teenager spanking is clearly not recommended.

Just as for spanking, if raising one's voice is used on very rare occasions then the parent will find it somewhat effective. Used once in a while, for selectively important instances, a parent's yelling can bring a youngster back in line. There is no clear definition for "rarely," the parent is urged to exercise good judgment for when a raised voice may serve as a beneficial, constructive purpose. More than three or four times a year is too often because yelling can also make a teenager tense. Such tension is emotionally unhealthy for a developing youngster.

General Principle #4

The best methods of punishment are neutral, which means as little person to person interaction as possible. This principle minimizes the risk, as discussed earlier, of socially reinforcing the very behavior the parent is trying to eliminate. For young children the technique that best meets this criterion is called Time-Out. Parents are encouraged to review early childhood books that discuss the proper use of time out. However, for teenagers the use of time out in the home setting is inappropriate. It has been used successfully with teenagers in institutional settings, but for use at home it is judged to be treating a teenager in an immature manner. One of the main reasons for the development of the techniques outlined in this book is to overcome the trap of inadvertent social reinforcement. The techniques outlined minimize parent-child interaction while still applying strong discipline for inappropriate conduct. By reducing interaction over conflicts, battles between parent and child are drastically reduced.

Remember what I had said earlier about zero strokes. The most effective discipline techniques involve minimizing inadvertent stroking or interaction. The methods outlined later meet that criterion.

General Principle #5

No matter what method of discipline the parent uses, no matter how effective the research says it is, it will not produce any lasting gains unless the parent actively socially reinforces the child. This involves not only deliberate praise for specific improvement but also unconditional expressions of love and caring, which includes giving each child individual time for talking and for having fun. Without these ingredients do not expect to succeed.

Remember the principle of consistency for discipline. This principle is even more important for social reinforcement. Without reinforcement we will not achieve our most important goal, which is a close and loving relationship.

Chapter 3

How to Control the
Difficult Adolescent

Parental Rights

One of the most difficult things for parents to do is to let go. If we are going to allow our children to mature mentally and emotionally between the ages of thirteen and eighteen, then we must gradually, and increasingly, over the years, back away and let the teenager experience the consequences of their actions. Not only can we not control their every breath and thought, but the more we try to the more they will withdraw from us.

I believe that parents will derive considerable comfort when they fully understand that, just like a psychologist, most of what they do with their adolescent is teach. Through communication we try to impart our knowledge and wisdom. However, just as there are patients that refuse to learn and to modify their actions so too are there adolescents that may refuse to learn. We may have to allow them to eventually take their lumps before they decide to listen.

Parents are often heard to say, "Just give them time and they'll grow up." For most teens this may be true. However, for the troubled teen "time" may not produce a maturing effect on the teenager. From a psychologist's point of view other things are going on. Such as the fact that as the teenager gets older, parental expectancies change. The parents gradually treat the child differently. These changes usually involve the parents requiring the teen to become more responsible for their actions. The parents do not protect them as much. As a result, in order to survive, the teenager begins to fire the old brain cells and lo and behold their functioning starts to improve. We call this maturing. I would like to teach parents how to speed this process along to get the teen functioning a lot more responsibly a lot sooner.

It is important to separate and clarify the difference of parent-child responsibilities. The areas of responsibility between parent and child can be divided into two broad categories, (1) Home and (2) Life. Home means those actions and behaviors that affect everyone within the general household, namely parents, brothers, and sisters. Life means those actions and social behaviors outside the home, either presently, or in the future, that only affect the adolescent. Categories of Life issues include sex, drugs, school, career, friends, dating, rock music, and attendance at concerts. Arguments between the parents and adolescents frequently confuse or muddle the two categories. Conflicts regarding Life issues are usually moot. The parent often becomes aggressive in insisting the adolescent listen and do as they are told. If the adolescent refuses to listen there is probably very little the parent can do about it, and frequently fighting only drives the adolescent further away and ultimately into engaging in more rebellious acts. Such arguments also further disrupt the peace and harmony of the household. Parents that continuously seek to overzealously control the adolescent in Life issues will perpetually drive themselves to frustration. However, some adolescents do go to extremes and get into serious trouble with drugs, or do engage in delinquent acts, or do fail miserably in school. Under such extreme circumstances the parent must step in and take action. Guidelines for effective action will be discussed in later chapters. Most teenagers do not get into these things heavily, but most parents assume that they do. As stated repeatedly, love and communication are the most effective tools for helping their teenager deal with these realities. For the most part, in Life issues the parent can best teach by "influencing" instead of "forcing." By having a strong and caring relationship the parent increases the likelihood that the teenager will follow their lead.

If the parent is bogged down in fighting with the teenager over Home issues then effective communications over the Life issues will be interfered with. This chapter presents techniques for controlling the difficult adolescent in the Home, with the central goal of reducing parent-teenager conflict, and thus fostering better relations and better communications for Life issues.

The following section will present the program for working with the difficult adolescent at the basic level. Escalating levels involving strong consequences when changes fail to occur will be presented in later sections.

24

The Real Economy System for Teens
or
The R.E.S.T. Program

Level I

When setting up rules and regulations, whether in schools, business, or in families, I have found that an important key to success is to simplify. The more the rules, the more the complexities, and the more likely a program will fail. It took years to boil down the number of rules needed to control a teenager's behaviors to a mere four. These four rules cover basically what most parents want and expect from their teenagers.

The following four basic Home rules are all that are necessary for the teenager to follow in the R.E.S.T. Program. They are designed to represent responsible independent functioning that any mature teenager should follow without difficulty. If adhered to, they should eliminate most reasons for conflict between the parent and adolescent. Briefly the four rules of Home conduct are:

Rule #1 - Hygiene
Rule #2 - Chores
Rule #3 - Verbal and Physical Abuse
Rule #4 - Safety

Rule #1 - Hygiene:
Simply stated means clean room-clean kid by a specific time each day. This may sound simple but a lot of issues are involved. The clean room part means that a teenager is responsible each day for making their bed, hanging up their clothes, straightening their desk and shelves, and picking up miscellaneous "stuff" off the floor. Objects cannot be shoved under the beds, or behind furniture, nor in closets (which should be kept reasonably neat). One of the difficulties with this rule is the perfectionist parent that would enforce it to a ridiculous degree. Even with direct supervision it would be difficult for a therapist to teach good judgment, but nevertheless good judgment and reasonableness are vigorously counseled for parents. These programs

25

give the parents extensive powers and it is fervently hoped that parents will not abuse them. Good parenting entails a balance between not being afraid of your own child and not abusing your powers as a parent. A reasonably neat and clean room is all we are asking of the teenager. Quite sometime ago I listened to a counselor on a morning T.V. show advising parents that a teenager's room is their private domain, and that if a teenager wishes to live in filth they have the right to do so. The counselor stated that the parents should handle such a situation by simply keeping the door of the room shut. I wholeheartedly disagree with this position! I believe such a stance confuses the issues of a teenager's right to privacy with a parents' right to a clean home. Parents paid for the house, or apartment, every square foot of it, and therefore derive the right to have it kept as they wish. Parents should be able to entertain guests in an open home, and not feel they must hide in some deep dark corner because their adolescent son is a slob. Requiring a teen to keep a clean room in no way interferes with the teen's right to privacy.

Parents should not rifle through a teenager's drawers, belongings, letters, or diaries, etc. Privacy is a sacred trust. Just as parents would be furious if their teen went through their belongings, so too is the teen entitled to be angry if their private things are invaded. In our home even if a letter is left open no one looks at it without permission of the person to whom it belongs. We cannot expect a teenager to learn to respect the rights of others if we do not respect their rights. Parents often respond with the fear that their child may be into drugs, or something else equally horrifying. I believe it is important to wait until strong evidence becomes apparent before constantly searching for elusive evils. Actually, if a drug problem gets bad it is doubtful a parent will have to go through their child's belongings, since the problems will most likely become quite apparent.

The same idea of reasonableness, discussed before, applies to the clean kid rule. Some parents are very intolerant of teenage fads and often define faddish hairstyles and dress as unhygienic. Precise guidelines for dress codes cannot be given, but parents should be sensitive to the pressures teenagers are under to dress in the uniform of the day. Most of the time a teenager can easily be neat and clean and remain well within the adolescent fads, without resorting to extremes. In other words, it is O.K. for parents to set limits but neither the adolescent nor the parent should be excessive.

The clean room-clean kid rule does require firmness and in any home the parents are the final authority, judge, and jury. The parents are the boss, but we hope not abusively. Daily arguments by the teenager will not be allowed. It is important for parents to actively and openly listen to occasional assertions made by a teenager when they feel fairness has been violated. A teenager should not feel totally trapped by the program. They should feel that they can communicate with their parents when they perceive an injustice. Their parents do not have to agree, but should, at the very least, listen openly.

The time element means that the hygiene rule, i.e. clean room-clean kid, must be completed by a specific time each day. The best time is usually in the morning, on weekdays before leaving for school. On weekends allowances for sleeping-in late should be made. The reason the time should be specified for each day of the week is to avoid arguments because of confusion. Haggling over a few minutes, later turns into an argument over a half hour, and later over hours. Once this starts it does not seem to stop. The time is set and no deviance is permitted. The teenager knows the rules and the consequences. The teenager may not like this at first but once the fights with their parent subside I truly believe that everyone will feel considerably better.

The REST Program is designed to give more responsibilities to the teenager. In keeping with such a concept then the teenager should be fully responsible for their own time. This means no reminders, or warnings by the parents. It also means the teen should not be reliant on their parents to wake them in the morning. Parents are forever upset that the teenagers just do not think. Well they will continue to not think, to not pay attention, and to lack vigilance if we (parents) serve the role of professional reminder machines. Why should a teenager think when they have us to serve them so well. Most teenagers are perfectly capable of setting their clocks and waking themselves. After all this period of time is supposed to be preparation for adult life. Just like adults, experiencing the consequences of not being on time for work a few times either shapes appropriate behavior or leads to painful failure. The teenager will also learn after a few forgetful or lazy incidents when the consequences of the program are brought to bare on them.

Rule #2 - Chores

One of the worst things we can do in raising our children is to do everything for them. Sometimes the best parenting is less parenting.

When we cater excessively to our children we may actually be handicapping them. We teach them to depend on others for accomplishing things that are often necessary for survival. When we do too much for them we are playing the role of Rescuer and therefore training our youngsters to become emotional Victims. Once the teen is trained to be a victim it then becomes an extremely difficult handicap for them to overcome in adult life.

By doing too much we foster laziness. After years of such training we turn around and corner the teenager by harshly accusing them of being lazy. It is a confusing, double binding message for the teenager when on the one hand we teach laziness and then on the other punish it. Conversely, one of the best things we can do for our children is to teach them to take care of themselves. Being able to take care of oneself, and not being lazy about getting things done, underlie the traits for "task independence." This means that a person can initiate and problem solve when confronted with complex jobs and tasks. Task independence is certainly a helpful characteristic if one is going to develop emotional independence. The two traits are not the same; one can be task independent, and still be quite emotionally dependent. However, task independence decreases the likelihood or at least the degree to which a person might become emotionally dependent. It certainly helps to learn to do things for oneself. It makes it extremely difficult, if not impossible, to be "task dependent" and develop emotional independence. The best age to teach teenagers to take the responsibility of chores is not at thirteen, but from the age of four or five. It is difficult to begin teaching such habits at an age when habit patterns are becoming firmly established. Teaching a child from age five, all the way through to their teens, can be a wonderful growing and shaping experience. Children can develop a great sense of pride and self confidence as they expand their repertoire of skills and become more and more responsible. If the parent puts in the energy early in the child's life then the parent reaps the benefits of not having to be a slave to their children later. If the youngster is presently task dependent then do not delay. Begin the new changes now, before it becomes even later.

Teach young children everything and anything you can, such as cooking, sewing, making a bed, shopping, cleaning, car repairs, house repairs, to (in the teen years) learning how to buy a house, buying insurance, banking skills, paying bills, and doing a household budget. As stated earlier the school systems tend to be elitest and few children will be formally taught these skills. If the parents do not teach the teen all this early then in adult life they may experience considerable setbacks for being so ignorant. By the time a child is seven they should be making their beds and cleaning their rooms, and dressing themselves, as well as doing several of the major chores such as doing laundry, vacuuming, cooking, baking, and so forth. Teach boys and girls all of these things and do not worry about sex role confusion. These are not the elements that make for sexual identifications. As a matter of fact children will learn to be more secure with their sexual identity if they learn they can comfortably do all of these things without constant worrying about their image.

When parents and children learn to work side by side and share responsibilities then a special closeness develops. It can foster the early development of a pattern of adult to adult communications. Such a relationship is more conducive to authentic intimacy than are yelling, screaming, or pleading.

If doing chores was not begun during the pre-teen years, then at least get started when they are a teenager. The chore rule means that the teenager is to do at least one major chore and several minor chores each day of the week. The chores are to be done without reminding them. Coaxing, pleading, yelling, or any such negative forms of interaction are out because these are exactly the kinds of communications that interfere with the positive type of parent-child relationship we are striving for. Instead, let the consequences of the program (to be outlined shortly) do the work for you. When you keep after the teenager to fulfill their responsibilities they only see you as "being on their case." They identify you as the problem and do not see it as their neglect of responsibility. The more you try to point out their shortsightedness the more they externalize the blame, directing it at you and staying angry at you. The consequences for not thinking will be automatic for the teen once the program is started. They will clearly know the rules of the game, and it is very difficult to blame anyone else when they goof up. They will begin to understand how they earned the consequences by their actions. Mature, responsible patterns of thinking will begin to emerge.

When there is more than one teen in a family then major chores should be rotated on a weekly schedule between them for fairness. Parents should also participate in major chores and not make the teens slaves. It is important to not go from one extreme to another. Do not "use" your teenager.

Rule #3 - Verbal and Physical Abuse

This rule is aimed at dealing with what I observe to be the most commonly presented complaint when parents drag their teenager into the office. Verbal abuse is quite common and often is the major source of parental frustration. Physical abuse toward a parent is rare, but it certainly does occur.

Included in verbal abuse are the sarcastic tone of voice, hate stares, and eye rolls which seem to say that they wonder how you ever made it to middle age without the entire world collapsing. Also included are cursing and various cruel statements, such as "drop dead." Constant oppositional challenges to everything you say and every request you make are abusive. Threats such as "I'll run away" are part of the teen abuse repertoire.

I honestly believe more kids are verbally abusive to parents today than at any other time in history. Psychology may in large measure be responsible for making parents afraid to take a stand and put a stop to inappropriate child behavior. The parents have been made to fear emotionally scarring their children by saying "No." Often it is the parents who are required to do the adjusting. It is the parents that learn to adapt by learning to tune out their child's offensive behaviors, while the child is allowed to go on and on. For goodness sakes our children "need" structure. It is the absence of structure that is emotionally unhealthy for them.

Abusive statements are not only no longer to be addressed to the parents but also to any other members of the household, including brothers and sisters. Yes, siblings will bicker and fuss with each other, and for the most part it is best to allow youngsters to fend for themselves. This means that when occasional conflicts between siblings occur it is best to stay out of it. Children must learn to take care of themselves, and for the most part it is best for the parents to stand back and let them work it through. However, when sibling conflict is frequent and persistent then the parents may have to step in to help bring it under control. When the conflict reaches aggressive proportions, with threats of aggression or with actual physical violence, then the parents should indeed intervene. A good rule of thumb for parents is let the kids deal with the problem themselves as long as there is not threat or occurrence of violence, and as long as it does not disturb the peace and serenity of the parents.

If the parent judges they must intervene in a sibling fight it is important to avoid the "He said - She said" controversy. This means do not go charging into the room saying "What's going on here?" I promise all you will hear is a confusion of accusations and cross accusations. "He's using my computer when I need it." "She said I could use it on Saturday mornings. Besides, she's been on the phone all morning." Etc., etc., ad nauseum. The parent finds themselves in the People's Court playing Judge Wapner. This approach not only does not settle the conflict, but gets you right in the middle of it. To avoid being trapped, the ongoing rule is that if you must step in, then both kids,

30

or all parties get punished - without questions being asked. They will soon learn there is little percentage in frequent or severe fighting. One additional problem is also taken care of. The younger children often become professionals at goading the older kids into reacting and then they victoriously plead the role of the injured party while you punish the older and more apparent culprit. That is not fair. This rule takes care of both the goader and the goadee.

When given the power to control aggressive verbal patterns the parent must remember not to restrictively trap the teenager from all forms of expression. It is important to allow assertive expressions for defending their self interests and rights. A teenager does not miraculously learn appropriate verbal behaviors. Yelling and screaming at them for their aggressiveness not only does not teach them proper behavior, but paradoxically models the very verbal patterns you are trying to eliminate. The training in proper verbal patterns can best be accomplished by setting automatic consequences where inappropriate verbal behavior is punished and rewarding proper verbal assertions. The rewarding of assertions are best accomplished by active listening. It is essential that the parent put energy into trying to understand and interpret what it is the teenager is trying to communicate. When a parent says "No," then it is important that they can clearly identify why they are saying no, i.e., what are their reasons. If you do not clearly and sensibly know why you are saying no, then you are abusing your parental powers and discouraging your child's assertiveness. Sometimes a little honest self-examination does not hurt.

When we refuse to listen and we continuously suppress a teenager's attempts at asserting we can expect these appropriate verbal patterns will extinguish, and in its place will be substituted either non-assertive and/or aggressive patterns. Only when their assertions meet with a fair amount of success will the teen be encouraged to continue them.

Rule #4 - Safety
Teenagers tend to be reckless. In most cases they have not come to grips with their fragility and mortality. It is not unusual to see them drive cars carelessly, and often it is while drinking or taking drugs. They may tend to go to dangerous places in the inner city with little concern for their well being. Staying out until the wee hours of the morning appears to be a weekend tradition. Parents can easily be found every weekend sitting up late waiting for their youngster to come wandering in. One of the greatest sources of parental frustration is trying to get our young to appreciate the danger with which we are so realistically familiar.

31

Firmly stated, we as parents are still responsible for our children's safety until they are eighteen! Therefore, the Safety Rule requires that when the teenager goes out they return on time and that they call to check in if they change or deviate from their planned activities. If the car breaks down they are to call as soon as they can get to a phone. If they unexpectedly move from one party to another, they should call home to let their folks know where they will be. If they are late because the friend who owns the car and is driving for the evening refuses to leave, they should call home. If they have been drinking and are the primary driver then they should call their parents to come pick them up.

We, as parents should not have to sit at home agonizing. We at least have the right to know our youngsters' where-abouts. Perhaps there is not a great deal we can do in the event of danger. However, this rule can at least minimize some of our risks and can give us a little peace of mind. Sometimes our children do not know how much we love them.

As you already know I do recommend firmness but we do not have to be overly strict when setting a curfew time. When we make the time to come in too prohibitive we can cause difficulty for the teenager. If their friends have permission to stay out later and we require them to be in early, such as 11:00 p.m., then they will experience considerable consternation and pressure from their peers. If there is only one car then their friends will be angry at them for imposing your rule on all of them. If it continues time after time your teen may begin being excluded from invitations. Parents, be fair. Give them a reasonable time, do not box them into a difficult corner. I have little trouble with a 12:30 a.m. or 1:00 a.m. time limit on Friday or Saturday nights for fifteen or sixteen year olds. For certain special occasions even a little more leniency would not hurt. But, once the time is agreed upon, it is strictly enforced

Enforcing the Rules
Consequences for Level I in the REST Program:

As stated earlier one of the major conflicts of the disrespectful, mindless adolescent is affluence. All they have to do is put their two feet on the floor each morning and they are surrounded with an abundance of material comforts. They learn that material wealth is like the proverbial money tree, it is always there. No thought, no effort, no planning, no sacrifices are necessary. When the mind and body are not used we can think of them as atrophying. If this is what we do to the teen then no wonder they can gravitate to a low level of functioning. Why should they think or behave?! The usual scenario between parent and adolescent involves the parent yelling, screaming, pleading, and begging and then buying their child a stereo. Then the parent yells, and screams some more and then pays for an exhorbitant phone bill. Some more yelling and some more major purchases. This goes on endlessly for years and years. Such a continuous sequence of events gives our power away. No one wins in this situation. After all, we are in actuality abundantly reinforcing the adolescent for the very misbehaviors we are trying to make them stop. The parent feels angry and frustrated, and usually feels like a slave to their own child. The children equally feel angry and frustrated for being picked on so much; they learn nothing and they do not change. All in all it seems quite counter-productive. So why do we keep doing it? Perhaps because we know of no other alternative. The REST program gives us a healthy alternative.

The idea behind enforcing the Level I Program is to require the adolescent to earn their resources by complying with the Four Rules of Conduct. Instead of rewarding them for misbehaving, let us reward them only for proper conduct.

The guiding principle does not involve something to the effect of "If you get good grades I will buy you something special, like a car" approach. I view such an approach as bribery on the part of the parent and extortion on the part of the teen. Such an approach teaches very questionable values. The REST Program does not involve buying anything extra, and does not involve any additional expenses. Simply stated in the REST program the teenager will be responsible for all their resources. They will henceforth earn what we are now giving them. If they wish to go without, then all they have to do is misbehave. If they wish to have nice things then they must behave.

To start, the parent estimates how much money they have spent on the youngster in the previous year for everything, including: shoes, socks, underwear, clothes, toys, games, records, make-up, concerts, lunch money, sports events, sports equipment, school supplies, camping equipment and entrance fees, car insurance, car payments, gas money, and everything else you can think of; the only two exceptions are food and rent - that we at least give them. Go through your check book and add your total - I hope none of you faint from this exercise. Becoming so clearly aware of how much we spend on our youngsters can be quite shocking. It is risky to give a specific figure to help you since there is a long lag between writing and publication, and the conditions of the economy can change drastically. However, just to give you a little help, by the standards existing right now in a middle class suburban community a teenager's expenses can run between $30.00-$40.00 per week for a thirteen year old, to $60.00-$80.00 for an eighteen year old. Please remember that by the time you read this these figures will most likely be outdated.

The parent will give the teenager a daily allowance for complying with the four rules. The allowance is not extra windfall money, but instead is money that will be required if the teenager is to have any resouces other than food and a place to live. They will hence earn everything that had formerly been given them freely. The daily allowance is calculated as close to their basic need level as possible. Therefore, they have to work hard to meet their weekly total. The amount earned daily should be slightly deficient for the teen to have everything they deserve. The difference is made up as a bonus for seven perfect days of earning the daily allowance. For example, if a fourteen year old receives $35.00 per week - then they earn $4.00 per day, which totals $28.00 for seven days. Not quite enough. If they earned their allowance seven straight-perfect days they receive a $7.00 bonus to equal the $35.00 for the week. Thus, the only way they can avoid a state of deprivation is rigorously keep up with the program. The allowance must be administered daily. This is essential in order to allow the teenager that slips a chance to get back on track as quickly as possible. By having a daily allowance, rewards match behaviors on a more consistent schedule. Also doing it on a daily basis the teenager that tries to be resistant soon finds themselves without financial resources for a weekend or lacking extra funds for a pair of badly needed jeans. With this program highly resistant teenagers usually cannot continue to be oppositional for more than three weeks before they find themselves in financial desperation. Any further attempts at resistance will only be injurious to themselves. Remember, all that is being required of them is to be a responsible and well behaved person.

The allowance should be given in cash late in the evening, let us say around 10:00 p.m., in an envelope placed on their night table. If they have failed in even one rule then instead of the allowance the envelope contains a note which clearly defines which of the four rules the child has broken. The note not only serves as behavioral feedback but also serves as a neutral means of communication. In this way the parent cannot be identified as "being on their case." When you verbally point out what they have done wrong the teen interprets this as you being on their case. The note circumvents this problem. It stops the incessant arguing. The parent also avoids inadvertently socially reinforcing the child because it minimizes personal interaction. Furthermore, the note serves as an effective means of reaching the child who has learned to tune a parent out. If the child feels the contents of the note are unfair then the next day they may request a conference to discuss the issue - but only assertively. They may not argue aggressively, if they do, they lose their allowance for the next day too. Again, parents are counseled to be fair, but not unnecessarily soft.

The note should be clear and concise, a 5" x 7" index card would serve well. They should state which rule(s) have been broken, and where, when, and how. For example:

BROKEN   **REASON**

Rule #3 -   Talked in a nasty tone to me in the kitchen after school when asking about party for the weekend. Refused to listen to my reasons for No.

Rule #2 -   Minor chore not done. Towels and underwear left on bathroom floor in a.m.

I am aware of the criticisms in the use of a note, perhaps the most frequent is the complaint of not using a direct method of communication. Remember, we are dealing with the difficult teenager - not with just any and every teenager. We are dealing with the teenager that refuses to operate on a direct adult communication level. If it is possible to directly communicate verbally, fine I have no qualms with that. However, if that fails, I find the note method works nicely.

Some parents may also complain that if they give their youngster so much money they will use it on drugs or frivolous things. That may be quite correct. If a child is seriously into drugs or alcohol then a more advanced program known as Tough Love should be used. Tough Love will be discussed later. The REST program is primarily designed to deal with teenagers that are not seriously into chemicals but who are difficult to control and to live with at home. If they are using the money for chemicals or other frivolous things then there will not be enough money left over for the basic needs, and soon enough the teen will feel an incredible pinch. In fact, this program makes it more difficult for the teen to buy drugs or other luxury items. When the parents are providing all a youngster's needs then spare money can easily be squandered on drugs and junk. It is actually easier for a teenager to buy chemicals when all their basic needs have been taken care of.

The REST program requires that the teen quickly learn responsible financial management. It incorporates the very same responsibilities we must live with as adults. Careless management of money leads to a very painful state of periodic deprivation. Such consequences are automatic for us and so should they be for the teen. Nothing will encourage mature thinking and attitudes more than real life consequences for immature thinking and attitudes. Additional meaningful financial management skills also can be developed. The teen becomes acutely aware of the need to learn how to budget within a fixed income. When the parent did the buying it was nothing to demand designer names for jeans, shoes, shirts, etc. and still they were able to go to concerts on weekends. I have noticed with keen interest that many teenagers that I have had on the program began looking more practically and sensibly at the purchase of sturdier and less expensive clothing items. They began cutting back on frivolous expenses. The parents actually wind up saving on hidden luxury expensive items and the teenager develops a sense of consumer wisdom. The need to learn financial management skills is further enhanced by the additional rule of NO LOANS. Once the teenager is out of money they are out. Loans not only prevent the youngster from learning to control their spending but completely neutralize the effectiveness of the program. A cash advance will lead the youngster to stop keeping the rules for a while. Once the loan has been depleted any money they earn then has to go to repaying the loan. This leads to a "why bother," defeatist attitude and then the parent is trapped with an unmotivated teenager.

One day each week should be scheduled for banking. This is the day the youngster banks any money left over into an operating savings account for future larger purchases. This also takes excess money out of circulation that may be spent frivolously and also emphasizes the savings habit. When teenagers have accumulated extra cash in the house there is a big chance they will temporarily stop performing on the program at least until all cash is depleted. This leads to a very sporadic pattern of compliance and can be rather discouraging for the parents. So, excess cash is best taken out of circulation each week.

When a major purchase is needed by the teenager the parent takes them shopping in the usual manner, but the teenager either draws the money from savings or writes a check from their own account.

The issue of bank accounts is important. It is somewhat complicated by the reluctance of some banks to handle teenage accounts. The most preferable arrangement is for the teenager to have a checking and a savings account. The parent has joint access to be used only for emergencies. Having a checking account is a very adult thing and teenagers often respond more maturely when performing such a symbolically adult behavior. The checking account is used for all operating transactions, including the accumulation of funds for major purchases, i.e. the amount is allowed to build until a major purchase is made. The savings account is used for long range goals such as college. Withdrawals from savings are not allowed, except under very unusual circumstances and only with parental consent. Windfall money, such as cash gifts from relatives, are also deposited into the Long Term Savings Account and should not be used to undermine the program.

In some locations a large deposit is required to open a teenage checking account and a basic sum must be maintained at all times. This creates a reserve that a teenager can draw from without prior notice to the parents. This would not only undermine the program but would make it tempting for the teenager to easily overdraw their account without having to pay the penalty of overdraft notices from the bank. Under those conditions it is best to have two separate and distinct savings accounts. The first account substitutes for the checking account and is used as an Operating Savings Account for deposits and withdrawals for all purchases, and the second account remains the same Long Term Savings Account as described above.

Parents should exert as little control as possible over the adolescent's expenditures. They will learn the price of fiscal responsibility a lot faster from the consequences of being broke and from bank overdraft notices than they will from you yelling at them. Let the program not only control their behaviors at home but also let it control how the youngsters learn to manage money. Stop yelling, stop getting your physiological system all worked up, stop destroying your relationship with your child; relax and be patient, the program will do the work for you. Let them experience the consequences of thoughtlessness and irresponsible behavior; they'll grow up a lot faster that way.

Super items, that are major purchases such as computers and trips to camps, should be handled in a slightly different way. If the teenager asks for a super item such as computers, stereos, mopeds, etc. and if the family can afford it and wishes for the youngster to have it then do not give it to the teenager, let them work for it. This adds considerable power to the effectiveness of the program. Simply add the amount of the item onto the daily allowance and stretch it out over several months. The extra amount is immediately set aside and saved toward the purchase. The more the youngster does not cooperate, the longer it will be until they can buy what they so desperately cannot live without. As an example, if the teenager wants a printer for their computer at a cost of $600.00 and the parents feel it is a worthwhile item, then add an amount such as $5.00 a day to the basic daily allowance. Of course, when earned, the $5.00 is immediately set aside and saved exclusively for the printer. It cannot be used for operating expenses. Theoretically, the youngster could then earn the computer in 120 days, which is quite fair. By working hard over so long a period the youngster begins to learn the value of such items. They begin to understand what you must go through to scrimp and save in order to provide such luxuries for them. I believe they may even appreciate you a lot more after such lessons become meaningful to them.

Gifts for holidays and special occasions, such as Christmas, Hanukkah, or birthdays, often present a problem. Not to detract from the specialness of the occasion, gifts should certainly be given. However, at the same time we do not want to undermine the effectiveness of the program. Therefore, any gifts that fulfill the youngster's basic needs would interfere with the program and therefore should not be given. Any gifts that represent items they badly want should also not be given. Instead such gifts should be used as goals for which they must work. It is best to give gifts that are luxury trinkets which are pleasant and fun but do not interfere with the program, for example jewelry, wallets, purses, etc.

Instructions to the Teenager

There are three parts to the instructions. First is the introduction of the basic goal of the program, which is to change certain behaviors. When initially introducing the program to the teenager try to use as positive and as assertive language as possible. Do not say "I am putting you on this program because you've been lazy and miserable." Try instead, "We've been arguing a lot. I love you and I don't feel good when we fight. I also want to try to stop picking on you so much. We (parents) feel this program will help motivate you to fulfill certain responsibilities without us having to stay on your case. It will also give you more money and greater responsibilities deciding how to use your money."

To improve the positive tone it is suggested that at the onset the parents extend the hand of peace by making a conciliatory gesture, such as offering to extend the weekend curfew deadline by a half an hour or an hour. By being so positive you avoid backing the teenager into a defensive corner of anger and harsh rebellion.

After a positive introduction, in part two, you simply present the

38

four rules. Discussion and clarification are essential as you present each rule. For example:

There are going to be four simple rules to follow. The rules are aimed at bringing peace to the house and stopping any confusion over what is expected of you. The first rule requires you to have your room clean, your bed made and that you be neatly and cleanly dressed by 7:30 each school morning. Saturday you may sleep late, but the rule must be met by 10:00 in the morning. Sunday we have to go to church so the time will be 8:30 in the morning.

Rule two means you will have at least one major chore each day of the week, plus you will have several minor chores each day. I have made a written list; please look it over and I'll be glad to explain anything that is confusing. The purpose of the chores is for you to share in family responsibilities. Both of us (parents) will also be doing a fair share of the work around the house.

Rule three requires you to speak in a proper tone of voice to us. The following will no longer be allowed: a sarcastic tone of voice, yelling, footstomping, hate stares, and eye rolls. We expect you to speak politely and respectfully to us. Refusing to talk to us will not be allowed.

Rule four is for your safety. We want you to be home on time, especially on the weekends. Your time on Friday and Saturday night is 1:00 a.m. We also want you to keep us posted on your where-abouts. We're not spying on you, its just a big comfort to us to know you're safe and that we can help in an emergency. Therefore, if you change plans you are to call us at any time and let us know where you are going.

This covers the basics and you may wish to expand and elaborate on other issues important to you.

Part three covers the consequences. Here the parent may try the following:

We would like you to have more responsibilities and that includes you learning to handle money. We are going to

39

give you a daily allowance of $4.00. You will get your allowance at 10:00 at night if all four rules have been met that day. Otherwise, you will get a note telling you why the allowance was not given. If you have seven perfect days, then Saturday you will get a bonus of $7.00.

We will be opening a checking account and a savings account in your name. We will have joint access to the account in case of an emergency. Your savings account is for college (or for when you complete high school). The checking account is for your expenses, which will include your lunches, your entertainment, your records, your clothing, your school supplies, everything except your food. You can save money by making your own lunches each day. Therefore, you will have to learn to save money for many things you want. If you would like, we will be glad to help you learn to budget. No loans will be allowed. Therefore, you will have to honor the four rules if you are going to be able to meet your expenses. If you don't, you will find yourself hurting for money.

We know this may seem strict to you but it gives you a lot more independence and hopefully will stop all the "fussing" at home.

Keep the initial instructions simple. Elaborate later. Give the youngster a chance to digest all this. Do not keep nagging the teenager to comply with the rules. This is exactly what you are trying to get away from. Let the evening note do the necessary communicating.

Jobs and Other Income

Stated succinctly, money from other sources must not neutralize the effectiveness of the program. Therefore, money for jobs such as cutting lawns, washing cars, or waiting on tables cannot be earned unless the teen has six perfect days at home that week. Their behavior at home comes first. I repeat, six days of complying with all the rules perfectly or they do not go to their outside job!

It may be necessary to have a calendar week from Wednesday to Tuesday so that by Tuesday of each week they can contact the people they work for on weekends that they cannot be there. This gives their employer a chance to find a substitute. If the teenager repeatedly does not meet their commitments it is likely they will lose their outside jobs and that is tough! We are not asking them to do anything difficult at home. If they are responsible enough to meet commitments with an employer, then they are also responsible enough to meet commitments with their parents.

The earned money can go into their active checking account to help with regular expenses. They earned it, it's allowed. This does not undermine the program since they must continue six days a week of compliance if they are to go to their jobs at all.

Level II

In most cases the program at Level I should work nicely to bring the difficult adolescent under control, and restore a more positive and communicative relationship between parent and child. However, it is not unusual to run into an adolescent that is bent on continuing to be inconsiderate. Indeed, there are teenagers that are so narcissistic that they care nothing for the rights of the people with whom they live. When Level I does not fully work it may become necessary to move to a Level with even stronger consequences.

I prefer to inform the teenager of all the levels and what they mean from the outset. I believe it is perfectly fair that they know what to expect. They also may not readily claim unfairness because they had never been told. Tell them at the beginning that if it is necessary to go to Level II they will be given one warning. If they fail to heed that warning immediately then Level II will go into effect for a minimum of one year. The terms are non-negotiable.

Level II sets the requirement that the teenager will have to earn their allowance a minimum six out of seven days each week to earn weekend privileges. In laymen terms they will be grounded each weekend they fail to meet criterion. Grounding is stricter than is usually applied. For Level II grounding means no use of the telephone, of the television or of the stereo. No social contacts are permitted. The teenager may read, they may talk with the family, they may stay in the house or in the yard, nothing else is permitted.

During Level II, the entire program of Level I is still in effect with the addition of weekend grounding.

Level II should be taken seriously before being put into effect. The teenager should be given every chance to comply with Level I. An acceptable level of compliance at Level I is an approximate success rate of earning their allowance an average of five out of seven days each week. A lower success rate is not considered acceptable, and eventually will lead to moving up to Level II.

The teenager is forewarned, once Level II is begun it remains in effect for a minimum of one year. Anything less than a year and the teenager will ride it out, just as they do traditional grounding, and trouble will only start all over again. Level II is not entered into lightly, but the highly rebellious teenager must learn the lesson that you mean business and that you will not repeatedly grow soft and back down. Only under such circumstances will they get the message that they must behave.

Remember the grounding is only for a weekend. The teenager has a chance to get back on track as soon as possible. This is not traditional grounding with all its drawbacks that were previously discussed. In Level II the teenager may never be grounded for a weekend if they comply with the rules or they may be grounded each weekend if they stubbornly refuse to be decent to live with - the choice is theirs.

One additional note. The teen is forewarned that if they use anything that they are not supposed to during the weekend grounding such as, the stereo or telephone, then that item is lost to them for one full year.

Level III

The choice to go to Level III is made if Level II fails. Failure at Level II is marked by the teen not earning weekend privileges more than fifty percent of the time within a three month period. Going to Level III means the teenager is very badly out of control and the parents seem powerless to bring them within reasonable limits. Level III simply means sending the youngster to a boarding or military school for one year. After a year they may return home only if they will comply with the rules of Level I.

There are some strong issues surrounding Level III. I am choosing a boarding school setting for disposition as opposed to an inpatient adolescent psychiatric facility. Such facilities are becoming increasingly popular across the country and in general I find the lay public seeking help for their young to be quite misinformed about these programs.

I do not rule out enrollment of a teenager in a Psychiatric Adolescent facility. My thinking on the issue is that for a "truly" mentally disturbed child, manifesting symptoms of psychosis, of a severe depression, or of marked personality disorder such hospitals may serve well for the initial treatment. For a child addicted to drugs or alcohol hospitalization may be imperative. When suicide or homocide appear to be an immediate danger then commitment to a Psychiatric facility is indeed important. However, for an acting out, misbehaving teenager I prefer to exhaust all outpatient procedures before subjecting a child to such hospitalization. I think it is wrong to take a child's freedom away from them so readily simply because they have been misbehaving.

One of the main reasons for readily hospitalizing teenagers has been the scarcity of outpatient treatment techniques that work. One of the central purposes of my writing this book is to add to the kinds or procedures therapists may utilize on an outpatient basis. Often the therapist is at a loss over what to do with a child that cannot be reasoned with. Hospitalization is frequently the therapist's catchall answer when they can find no other tools to help do the job.

Parents should ask many questions before consenting to hospitalizing their child. First, when hospitalization is recommended seek a second opinion from a psychologist or psychiatrist that has no affiliation with the hospital being recommended. Take the time and trouble to have your child examined by another doctor. Admitting a child into a psychiatric unit is a serious decision that requires careful consideration.

I believe that while we may wish it were not so, there still remains a stigma to psychiatric hospitalization. Sometimes the long range psychological scars to a youngster of institutional hospitalization may outweigh the immediate benefits. Often a prescription for admission is simply done out of the doctor's frustration of not knowing what to do with the difficult youngster. Even the use of Tough Love should be weighed carefully. While I praise the Tough Love innovation I believe that it, along with hospitalization, should be used as last resorts and the methods of individual outpatient therapy, conjoint family therapy, and the procedures outlined in this book should in many cases be exhausted first. This hierarchy of treatment modalities, I hope, will considerably lessen the number of children that will ultimately require hospitalization.

There is an increasing trend to expand outpatient care as a more economically feasible means of treatment. Cost should also be a major consideration for all of us. Hospitalization is expensive. Either the direct costs are expensive or the inreases in insurance premiums will be passed to us. Outpatient treatment is a considerably cheaper alternative. As consumers we need to be aware of this. A $75.00 session with a therapist each week is considerably less expensive than a $500.00 per day hospital stay for several months. We as consumers of insurance pay for these exorbitant rates - it is part of "our" premium payments.

Chapter 4

Special Problems
Lying and Aggression

Lying is fairly common among teens while aggression appears to occur less frequently. For both of these behaviors there are degrees of severity. Minor levels of lying may be committed by the teen to cover up a clandestine, unapproved meeting with a boyfriend or girlfriend, or to hide drinking or smoking pot at a party, or to avoid a scene over a bad school grade. This happens occasionally and it does not mean the youngster is ill or disturbed. However, frequent lying over many trivial things during the course of a week, and maintaining a hidden world from his or her parents may mean the child is quite disturbed or that the family as a whole may be functioning in an unhealthy way. If this is the case then we may be dealing with more serious emotional problems. However, in the vast majority of cases it is typical, although unfortunate, that adolescent misbehaviors are not indicative of some serious disorder.

When lying occurs the parents are quick to point the finger at the youth and then drag them into the therapist's office to have the problem "fixed." Often, however, it may turn out that lying is the end product of poor family communications. A youngster may develop the habit of lying to avoid dealing with excessively punitive parents who severely and frequently discipline every minor infraction. Such parents often do very little listening but instead rant, yell, and dictate, forcing the teenager to go underground and lie. The youngster then learns to function covertly and is reinforced by escaping constant harassment and punishment. Parents must learn that if they want the teen to openly communicate then they best be prepared to hear exactly what they do not want to hear. The parent does not have to approve of everything the teen says and does, in fact they can openly disapprove of the teen's behavior but without the yelling, screaming, and constant threats of grounding. The teen has to learn that Mom and Dad may not like what they do but at least they can tell their parents what is going on in their head. Open communication increases the chance that the

47

parents may reach the teen. If the teen is forced to keep everything hidden then there is no chance for parents to influence any of their behavior.

To foster better communication and decrease lying the therapist may recommend conjoint family sessions where all members have a group session and practice discussing issues. The therapist then acts as a mediator and teaches good communication skills.

I have also found that some teenagers lie because they do not like or respect their parents. Sometimes this is the product of distorted perceptions of the parents on the part of the teen. Through individual therapy they may change their views. Unfortunately, often there may be considerable legitimacy to the teen's point of view and lying is a way for them to avoid dealing with someone they simply do not like. I have often met parents that behave inappropriately where they may exercise poor judgment in many aspects of their lives and may behave hysterically and overreactively. I can remember cases of parents that scream and yell and pound the dashboard of the car in the presence of their entire family simply because the car would not start immediately. I have even had extreme cases where the parent cross dresses as a transexual in the home and then is surprised and upset because their children do not respect them. When cases such as this occur the focus of therapy may turn out to be with the parent rather than with the teen. If the parent truly judges himself to be an honest and reasonable person and the youngster persists in habitual outrageous lying then the sooner steps are taken to change the teen's behavior the better the chances to break the habit. The techniques are identical for dealing with aggressive behaviors and will be discussed shortly.

One further note. It is important to correct the habit of lying early in a child's life. In fact, correction is best accomplished before the teen years. As the years go by the habit can become conditioned quite strongly and therefore can become increasingly resistant to being broken. Furthermore, to correct lying, parents must be able to detect when the child is indeed lying. As the teenager continues this habit they may become too skilled for the parent to detect even a slight trace of a cover up. It is therefore important to correct it while you can still pick up on it, that is while the child is young and a far less sophisticated liar.

Aggressive behaviors can be defined as encompassing physical violence directed either toward another person or toward immediately surrounding objects. It is the manifestation of almost complete loss of impulse control. It can be expressed as hitting someone, throwing objects, kicking or punching walls, or pounding fists on the furniture.

Aggression is classified as a low frequency behavior. This means that even in very aggressive children it usually does not happen all that frequently. The aggression may occur two or three times a year or it may happen several times a week. It is a dangerous behavior, someone can really get hurt, and it should be stopped immediately. Do not assume the child will grow out of it. It does not work that way. Explosive rage reactions do not stop automatically when we reach eighteen or when we walk down the aisle to say, "I do." Habits do not change because we grow older chronologically, in fact they become more ingrained. If a behavior is expressed consistently throughout youth there is a high likelihood it will persist throughout adult life. Even if no one is physically hurt rage reactions destroy relationships and can be extremely emotionally scarring to a developing youth.

Interestingly many teens learn aggression from their parents' behaviors. Often the parents model aggression and modeling is one of the most powerful methods of teaching. Therefore, one generation seems to pass on violence to the next generation. Abusive adults often come from abusive parents.

If you are an explosive parent do not expect your child to stop unless you do. You will need to face this and probably professional help will be needed to break the habit.

Sometimes traditional methods of therapy are effective in teaching patients, whether adults or teenagers, to begin learning emotional restraint and to begin to bring the problem under control. However, I have found that once the habit is well ingrained in a teenager or in an adult it is extremely difficult for them to break. Traditional methods of therapy often do not seem to be of much help. Patients may try to control themselves for a while but eventually stress or a trigger situation will start it again. I am often amazed at how difficult it is for people that have rage reactions to stop.

The key to controlling lying and aggressive reactions is to increase the person's motives to control the behaviors to a level that surpasses the temptation to misbehave. When confronted with stress the perpetrator usually loses control. Only when the "external" rewards and punishments are great enough can the person find the inner strength to exert some self control over these behaviors. Fortunately, in dealing with teenagers it is relatively easy to control the rewards and punishments. We usually have been giving this power away. The teenager that lies and acts violently often can be found to have a portable stereo, a ten-speed, a car, a personal T.V., etc., etc. They continuously misbehave and continuously receive rewards.

To deal with lying and aggression we will add the following steps

49

to the Level I program which continues to remain in effect. The procedure is easy to implement. Stay on the regular Level I program for the four basic rules and simply add the following steps. Identify six to ten objects or activities that are most important to the teenager. Write a list of these in rank order, i.e. from the most favorite item to the least of the favorite items. An example might be:

1. use of the family car -------------------------Most important
2. guitar
3. stereo
4. dirt bike
5. personal telephone
6. personal black and white T.V.
7. home computer ------------------------------Least important

Then inform the teenager that each time there is a major transgression of either a lie or a violent act one item will be removed for exactly one year. Note on paper the starting and ending dates. Start with the lowest item on the list. In this instance the home computer would be lost first. Each additional infraction means the loss of the next item up the list.

Notice this is designed for the noose around the neck to pull tighter and tighter the more misbehaving continues. In my private practice, most teenagers who engaged in lying or violence only tested one or two items before stopping, and stop they most certainly did. Only a couple of teenagers went all the way up to item one. One of them whose parents had a history of inconsistency admitted that he did not believe his parents would follow through. Once he was convinced they were now consistent he got the idea.

What if the child goes through the entire list and loses item #1? Inform the teenager that if item #1 is lost then we move to Level II automatically - and Lying or Aggression become rule 5 on the Level II program. Proceed right to Level III if Level II fails.

Chapter 5

Special Problems
Poor School Performance

The two greatest lies in the world are "Mom, the teacher never gives us any homework.", and "Teacher, I lost it on the bus."

Poor school performance is a huge issue and one of the most frequent presenting problems in private practice. The problem involves many complex issues. Issues I believe that parents and educators need to give some honest thought.

Before beginning a specific program it is crucial to determine "why" the child is failing. The same manifested behavior, in this case, poor grades, may have a multiplicity of causes.

First, I truly believe that not enough parents are encouraging their children to perform at their best in school and insisting that they take their education seriously. The modern generation of youngsters appear to have been trained to avoid frustration and struggle. It pains many parents to see their child sweat and labor over school which results in a message of "do as little as you have to and go out and have fun." This sets up a paradox of mixed messages. On the one hand parents cannot bear to see their child struggle but when Junior shows up with a poor report card all hell breaks loose. The parents cannot understand "what is the matter with that child." Then the screaming and yelling starts followd by two months of grounding. Parents need to learn that they must teach their children that success comes with hard work and sweat.

Parents must remember that they are not only teaching their children proper behavior but that they are, more importantly, transmitting values. How much you show that you care about your child's work shows how much you value education itself. If you don't get excited by your child's learning and scholarship, then why expect your child to develop such values. Ask yourselves if you take a deep interest in what your child has learned at school each day. Do you take pride in his or her daily accomplishments? Do you reinforce them for their daily efforts? Is their education at the center of importance in the

51

household? Or is school just something to get through until youth is over?????

When I was a school teacher in the 1960's, I learned a very important lesson. I saw the board of education's money pour into all types of sophisticated teaching equipment such as video cameras, programmed learning machines, computers, fancy rooms and so forth. What struck me was the realization that all this fancy stuff meant nothing if the child was not deeply committed, motivated and involved in their own education. Those children that were highly motivated would learn even without all the fancy equipment, all they would require would be the bare essentials of books, paper, pencils, and blackboards. The motivation a child has comes primarily from the family. All the fancy equipment does indeed enhance learning but it is not a substitute for the involved child. Parents stop passing the buck! You cannot expect your teenager to love school if in their early formative years you have not actively transmitted the value of a love for learning.

Educators must also reflect on their responsibility to the failing student. The key question is, "Are the needs of the child being met?" Many youngsters are not college bound. They have no interest in things academic. I have found that many of the students are interested in manual-vocational training. Yet, they are required to sit in classes that are beyond their interest. They may be in class bodily but their minds are elsewhere. What a waste of time and money when we cannot and do not excite their interest. Fortunately, more school systems are returning to the implementation of programs that are designed for such students. However, I wonder if we are going far enough soon enough.

I recall a Catch 22 situation I encountered with a teenaged patient just a short while ago. He was failing miserably in high school., He fervently stated his disdain for his abstract, academic courses. He felt terribly about himself. However, he could repair and rewire an automobile blindfolded. He loved working with his hands. We appealed to the county school board to transfer this student to one of the existing vocational schools. The youngster wanted to go in the worst way. Their reply was, "We cannot transfer poor students, only those with good grades can have the option." Try as I might I never succeeded in convincing the "authorities" of the importance of meeting the needs of a youngster who is failing. I am convinced that this youngster would have performed well in a vocational setting.

If a child has been doing poorly a few simple strategies should help considerably. Here are a few things a parent can do.

When asked by their parents how the grades are going many teenagers respond, "Fine, I'm doing pretty well." They honestly mean this even though their semester grade average may in fact be in the "D" or "F" range. Many teenagers have limited insight. If they did well on the last two or three quizzes in a subject they believe they are indeed doing well. They easily forget the grades of 40 or 50 from just two or three weeks earlier. If they were more acutely aware of their ongoing grades throughout the entire semester then they may realize the necessity for extra special effort to compensate for any previously weak performance. To help the child be more aware of ongoing performance all the teen needs to do is record all test and homework grades. The grades should be posted in a convenient location to serve as a constant visual reminder of where they stand at any given time. It is had to rationalize away the existence of a poor grade or two when they are staring you right in the face.

A sample recording sheet is provided in Figure 1. Photocopy the sheet, or draw a similar one. Begin a fresh sheet the start of each report card period. The youngster is then responsible for recording grades "every day." The parents should keep abreast of these grades "every day." Both parent and child should know precisely where the child's performance level is at any given time - no surprises at the end of the six weeks.

Another type of form is provided in Figure 2. This form is used to communicate with the parents on a regular basis the teacher's assessment of the teen's weekly performance. The form is to be filled out by the student's teachers every Friday. If each teacher's grade book has been kept up to date it should only take each subject teacher five seconds to check the appropriate columns and sign the sheet. Each Friday it is the student's task to take the form to each teacher for completion. Any missing entries and it is assumed the youngster did poorly for the week in that particular subject.

Notice the sheet is designed to look like a mini report card. That is exactly what it is - in an unofficial way. The child's performance can be monitored more consistently this way.

Sometimes I will hear teachers say they do not have the time to do this for all their students and will refuse to help. First, this is not done for all the students, only for the one or few students that are failing. Next, the teacher is legally responsible to meet the needs of each child. Teachers please remember it is only a few minutes of extra time but it can be an enormous help.

Students sometimes poke fun at a student that is on a program such as this. No one need know about the program except the student and his teachers. All the student needs to do is carry the sheet in a plain

Figure 1

SUBJECTS

GRADES

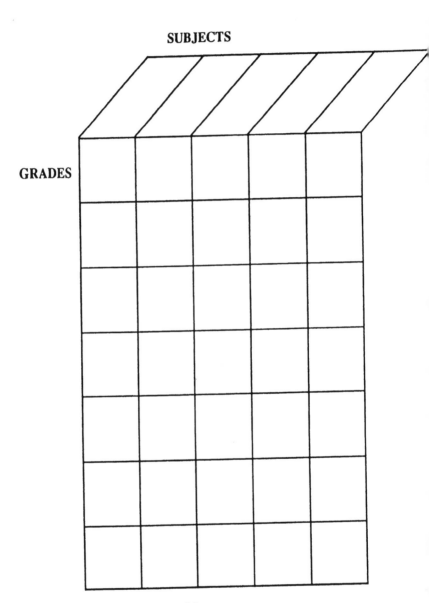

Figure 2

NAME: _____ DATE: _____

SUBJECTS	CLASS PERFORMANCE					CONDUCT				HOMEWORK				HOMEWORK ASSIGNED		TEACHER'S INITIALS
	A	B	C	D	E	E	S	N	U	E	S	N	U	YES	NO	
1.																
2.																
3.																
4.																
5.																
6.																
7.																
8.																
9.																
10.																
11.																
12.																

COMMENTS: _____

55

envelope and discreetly place it on the teacher's desk at the beginning of class and pick it up at the end of class. I have found that if other students find out about the program it is usually the student on the program who has started the rumor floating. The parent may have to meet with all the teenager's teachers at the beginning of the school year to explain the program. Show the teachers this text so they may understand the design and purpose of the program - it will save a lot of explaining. I have found most teachers like it. They find the approach sensible and they like it even more when they quickly see a failing youngster's grades going up. Rarely have I encountered a teacher that refuses to help.

Notice on the sheet that all aspects of the child's performance are assessed. Whether it is conduct problems, failure to do homework carefully, inattention in class, or poor class performance, all aspects are to be evaluated. Nothing should be left to chance. The teacher should have a weekly average for each area and then simply check the column that is closest to estimating the student's performance from Monday through Friday of "that" week only. Each week is a fresh start. After six weeks the sheets should closely match the report card grade. No surprises. Any inconsistencies need to be clarified. Was the teacher not keeping accurate records? Did the student forge any grades? Did the parents not check each week as they should?

The weekly report would be of little use if it were not tied into consequences. Remember yelling, screaming, hitting and even begging and pleading do not produce behavioral or additudinal changes and only serve to damage the parent-child relations. I am sure it is tempting for parents to want to get their dander up when a child is failing. We, as adults, know from experience how difficult life can be and how important school is for our jobs and careers. It is indeed frustrating when a youngster does not see it. Sometimes I recognize that out of love and concern we feel as if we could explode. Only, to do that is not constructive, and it does not work. Long range consequences of damaged career opportunities are often meaningless to a teenager. Yelling is often meaningless. So we must use what is meaningful to them. A tough stand on grounding each weekend has proven to do wonders for grades. Remember, going out and having fun are high on the priority list for teens. The grounding must only be for the weekend. The consequences are to be repeated each week. If the weekly report is conveniently lost let the teen know you checked the grades directly at school and they are grounded anyway.

To enforce each week's peformance set a specific criterion level. For example class performance can be set at "B" and no grade for the entire week may fall below "B" or they are then grounded for the weekend. Conduct and homework may be set at nothing less than "S" for the entire week. Any single grade below criterion means grounding that weekend. This is an "all or none" rule. If we allow one or two slippages because the child's grades are showing an overall improvement, in other words, if we get soft, then the teenager will calculate exactly how much he can get away with and rapidly gravitate to that level. Set the criterion and stick to it. Once you start giving an inch you can expect your child to take a mile. You are not being fair to your child by not being tough. I have found that if parents set criterion level at three "C's" a day, then they will get three "C's" a day. Of course it is important to judge as accurately as possible at what level your child is capable of performing. I find however, that most parents underestimate how well their child can perform. Once all the grades come up you will notice that you will have a much happier child.

The weekend grounding should be tough and thorough. It begins Friday night and ends Monday morning. The weekend should be as dull as possible. No television. No stereo. No telephone. No contact with friends. No shopping trips. No guitar. No use of either their car or of the family car. The use of a car can be one of the most powerful tools to motivate a teenager. The rule is to stay home, read, and play in the yard - but that is it. After the first grounding they will realize you mean business. All they have to do to prevent it is put some effort into their schoolwork. They may not like it at first but when their grades improve I believe you will see a vastly improved attitude.

If the teenager is caught using something which has been part of the grounding such as the stereo, then the item is locked in storage for one year. Warn them of this rule before beginning the program.

Explain the program in its entirety to the teenager. All types of responses are possible. Some youngsters readily welcome the program, wanting any push they can get to motivate them with school. Some youngsters will resent the program - but that simply is going to be the way it is. The decision to proceed is made without the youngster's consent. It is a unilateral decision made by the parents only. It is best to present the program in a positive way, reassuring your teenager that this is not punishment but a tough program to motivate them for improving schoolwork.

The grounding on a weekly basis is quite different than the typical parental method. It is enforced regularly for a relatively short period which allows the teenager to get back on track as soon as possible. The punishment is removed as soon as improvement occurs. In regular grounding the punishment usually stays in effect while the behavior

57

has improved. This ends up punishing any new efforts on the part of the teen. There is little chance with this program for a major lapse. In typical grounding six weeks go by before the parents have any idea what may be going on. In this approach no more than one week can pass before the parents are informed of school performance and consequences are enforced. Typical grounding usually allows an abundance of reinforcers to slip in such as telephone calls, television, etc. When enforcing this each weekend, extreme strictness must be adhered to, allowing little material reinforcement for poor performance.

Remember that while this program is in effect Level I program also remains in effect. The two programs are implemented side by side. The school program, once in effect, stays in effect for one full academic year. This allows the teen to develop the habit of a new, and higher, level of performance. If after removal grades begin to slip immediately put the program back into operation.

Instead of the typical scenario of yelling, screaming, and threatening, this program imposes meaningful consequences. The youngsters have learned to adapt to threats. They have learned to tune the parent out. They have learned that the threats have no meaningful substance to them, and that within a short time all will be forgotten and life will return to normal. All the teenager has to do is tough out a typical traditional grounding period. As a matter of fact, traditional grounding has become a status symbol among teenagers. It is a badge of honor among the peer group. Therefore they can ride out a temporary loss of material reinforcers. This program on the other hand is designed to impose consequences that do not let up. Consequences that mean a continued loss of social and material reinforcers will relentlessly be imposed on the teen until the teenagers finally decide to modify their school behavior.

Chapter 6

Special Problems
College

I love teaching in college. A college campus is the most exciting and stimulating environment I can imagine. I feel such joy from seeing many bright and eager faces. However, there is a drawback. Many students on almost any campus do, not belong in college. These are the students that party almost every night of the week, which is easy to do at most schools. These are the students that daydream in class, read their textbook for the first time the night before an exam, and blame everyone else, especially their professors, for their failure. These are the same students that are perpetuating the same poor habits and attitudes that they manifested in high school. Why, I often ask myself, are their parents investing about ten thousand dollars a year on such a youngster?

Parents often tell me that they are quite well aware of their youngster's immaturity but they are deeply concerned that their child will end up destitute and starving if the parent does not push them through a college education. What nonsense! All this does is prolong the child's immaturity. They barely benefit from any of their courses. The child's time is wasted. A precious space in college is wasted. What little return for a heavy financial investment.

By now the reader is probably well aware that the central and recurring theme of this book is accountability. Maturity and adulthood are achieved most quickly when we stop protecting our youngsters from the consequences of their thinking and their behaving. By overprotecting them we allow them to gravitate to the lowest level of functioning. When we overprotect them we not only allow immaturity, we actually end up reinforcing these behaviors and attitudes. When we lift the protective screen we begin requiring them to mobilize their resources and learn to survive. Parents are often amazed at what wonderful things their youngsters are capable of doing if we just stop babying them.

Teenagers do not begin maturing at age twenty-one simply because they have reached a new chronological stage. They begin to change because our attitudes and actions toward them start to change. We require more of them and we do less for them. We make them more accountable for their actions. We allow them to experience the consequences of their behaviors. As a result they begin to show signs of growing up. If "we" do not change them neither will they. I have seen many cases of emotionally crippled adults in their thirties who continue to function like early adolescents because their parents continue to over-nurture them.

Accountability also applies to a college education. Why should we be teaching them that you can do anything you want including failing repeatedly and your life will not change, i.e. there will be no consequences. You can continue on that beautiful campus even though you're getting "D's" and "F's". You can continue to play the most outlandish and unrealistic set of values and we will support you all the way.

I fervently submit to parents that an education is one of the most beautiful and cherished gifts we can ever give our youngsters. There is no education if it is just a warm body going through the system and not deeply committed. Education requires involvement, motivation, sacrifice, labor, and a total investment of oneself if one is to profit from the experience.

On the first day of classes each semester those students that do not know me are shocked when I announce that I do not take attendance. In fact, many parents are shocked. I tell my students that they are over eighteen and I fully intend to treat them as adults. I emphasize that I will assume they are in my room because they want to be there. I will continue to assume, until proven otherwise, that they "want" to learn and grow and that they do not have to be monitored like infants. Furthermore, I make it plain that I really prefer my room filled with eager minds and anyone that is bored, or tired from an all night bender is free to cut and stay in bed. I do not enjoy blank stares and yawns. I do not enjoy indifference. Not surprisingly, very few students cut and usually attendance is high.

Students' accountability comes into play by the fact that exams are based partly on lecture material; and partly on readings. Therefore, missing classes means not understanding what was taught. Judgment day comes with each exam. It is the students' responsibility to keep up with the course content. I do not see it as my responsibility to make or force another adult to do what is necessary.

If parents are dealing with an immature youngster and find themselves tearing their hair out trying to "make" their teenager enter college or stay in college when they repeatedly get low grades then why not consider an alternate approach. Why not consider holding off sending them to college until they are mature enough to benefit from such a heavy investment. Why not speed up their motivation by allowing them to experience the real and meaningful consequences of the real world.

If the teenager has demonstrated a lack of appreciation for school and has consistently maintained a grade poiny average below at least a "C" level with an overwhelming abundance of "D's" and "F's" then they are not ready for college. Helping them find a job and an apartment may be your best immediate alternative. Give them one or two months rent, even a downpayment for an apartment, and two weeks worth of groceries. Help them find a full time job. Then let them know in no uncertain terms they are henceforth on their own. Under no circumstances will you bail them out. If they do not pay their bills, let their credit rating suffer. If they cannot meet their car payments, it is their car that will get repossessed. Exactly what would happen to you if you did not meet your responsibilities? You may offer to lend your knowledge - if your youngster asks. You can teach them how to pay bills, how to manage a budget, how to deal with the banks, etc. However, under no circumstances will you pay anything for them or lend them any money.

Allow them to stay out in the cold for a minimum of one year. After that, if they truly realize the importance of improving their career profile and wish to enter college, let them know there is an open door policy and you will indeed help them "IF" they can convince you that they are ready. Do not encourage them, let them initiate the effort, let the burden of proof be on them, let them demonstrate sincerity. As further proof of their earnestness instruct them that they will have to contact the colleges for bulletins, applications, scholarships, etc. Let them problem solve. Let them learn to think.

When they do return to college set a rule that paying for their expenses will be on a semester by semester basis. If grades at the end of any semester fall below a "C" grade point average (2.0 on a 4.0 scale) then once again support will be withdrawn for one full year and then it is back to the apartment and back to the job market.

Parents that have a youngster already in college may also impose the same restrictions. Let them know before the next semester that you will no longer reinforce failure. You will no longer invest hard earned dollars in anything that continuously shows a poor return. Each semester's performance will determine entrance into the following semester.

Parents are often concerned that if they withdraw support their child will believe that their parents no longer love them. We often believe that an expression of love is to give and give and give totally and unconditionally. Neither of these assumptions is accurate. Why is it an expression of love to protect them from the real world? Why is it an expression of love to keep them functioning at an immature unrealistic level? Is it not the greatest expression of love to say it is time to get out of the nest and fly!

Chapter 7

Special Problems
Drug and Alcohol Abuse
Hardcore Behaviors

As stated in the beginning of this book, this text was not designed
to address the hardcore problems of teenage drug and alcohol abuse.
However, this psychologist is very impressed with the works of Pauline Neff, and Phyllis and David York, on the Tough Love approach. I
find this approach to be very consistent and compatible with the ideas
expressed in this program.

The basic concept of tough love is that it is not an expression of
love to allow your child to sink deeper and deeper in the pit of addiction. To force the youngster to stop chemical abuses the parent makes
it difficult to continue such behaviors. The authors refer to the idea of
no longer padding their corners. Which means to stop protecting them
and make them accountable for their actions. If the parents provide for
all their needs they then make life comfortable for an addiction. Drugs
and alcohol are expensive and if money is not used on subsistence then
it can be used to buy chemicals. If a youngster refuses to follow the
rules of the house and continues to abuse chemicals then in tough love
all support is removed. This includes not only money but also the roof
over their head. Time and energy must be used in the pursuit of survival intead of wasted in the pursuit of chemicals. The program strongly
urges parents to allow the youngster to experience the consequences of
their behavior, that is, to allow them to hurt. Only after hurting
enough may they then be motivated enough to modify their addictive
behaviors.

The pain of chemical addiction comes from multiple directions. It
comes from physical pain, when the nevous system rebounds in agony
from having been unhealthily suppressed. The pain can come emotionally, when the drugs wear off and the aftermath means profound
depression, anxiety, and fatigue. The work or school environment

63

adds to the pain as pressures mount from frequent latenesses and absences, and from a decline in performance. Social relations begin to fall apart. The addict cannot be relied upon or trusted in any way and therefore they become socially isolated. They seek other addicts for relationships, only they too cannot be trusted. Loneliness, emotional and physical pain, and financial pressures mount. Only when the pain outweighs the reinforcing effects of the chemicals will the addict be motivated enough to change. When fighting chemicals you are fighting an incredibly powerful demon. By removing support the parent speeds up the race toward "bottoming out." Parents experienced with having a chemically addicted teenager know that almost anything they try fails; pleading, crying, shouting, hitting, only reinforce the addict's distorted ability for self pity which leads to needing more drugs. Mental gymnastics. These distortions of reality are magnified when the youngster does not have to be concerned with food, shelter, clothing, and transportation. They can devote their full time and resources to the acquisition of chemicals.

In the Tough Love program parents learn that they are powerless over their youngster's addictive behavior. The only way the child will learn is to let them take responsibility for their actions. Parents are often frightened to let go, and this is indeed most understandable. They are afraid that terrible things will happen to their child if they do not continue to give them a protective environment. The parents must learn that terrible things are already happening to their children: they are killing themselves. Therefore, to help parents, support groups are often formed. Parents may derive strength from each other.

The support group also provides alternative safe havens for the teenager when a crisis is precipitated. When the parent is ready to confront the youngster, that is, if they are to stay home they must be chemically clean and they must abide by the house rules or else hit the door. If the youngster wishes to leave they can choose to go to a hospital drug and alcohol treatment program, or to one of the homes of a family in the support group, or to hit the streets. The choice is theirs. Of course, if they choose a support group family home, then the same rules are enforced there or confrontation immediately follows once again.

Because it is frightening for most families to go through the necessary steps by themselves I urge them to contact a tough love group in their community. Preferably one led by a licensed, qualified therapist. The parents and child enter separate groups. Both need support and both need therapy to get through this ordeal.

The chemically addicted teenager often seems as if they are possessed by demons. Rational behavior and normal reasoning are beyond what can be expected. The drugs alter their personalities and the quest to get the resouces to get the drugs dominates their behavior. Therefore, the parent is urged to implement Tough Love without delay and not proceed through the steps outlined in the REST Program. It is imperative to deal with the problem of the drugs first. They must be weaned off the drugs without delay and Tough Love confronts this head on. Furthermore, the REST Program puts money in the hands of the addict. Their ability to use any semblance of sense in managing their money has long since disappeared. Only one force operates - get drugs and indeed that is exactly where the money will go.

CHAPTER 8

Special Problems

Acting Out Behaviors
Runaway Reaction, Suicide Attempts
and Delinquent Behaviors
Hardcore Behaviors

These behaviors are the nightmares of many parents. A teenager attempting to end their life, or breaking the law, or disappearing to another city or state is, to say the least, frightening. When these behaviors occur the simplest rule is to immediately seek professional help. Do not try to deal with these actions on your own, forget your pride. There is too much at stake without a professional to guide you.

The first step a professional will take is to evaluate the reasons for such extreme behaviors. Such an evaluation is necessary because there are multiple and complex possibilities that have to be handled correctly if the risk factors are to be reduced to a minimum.

One possibility that must be entertained is the intent to emotionally blackmail the parents. "If you don't let me have my way look what I will do!" It is difficult to believe that a youngster would go to such lengths just to out manipulate their parents. However, as almost any therapist would assure you - indeed they do! This form of manipulation could be precipitated by attempt to resist the programs outlined in this book. Some children that do not like the program may resort to extremism just to get the parents to back off. A victory of this sort reinforces these extreme acts and therefore, increases the likelihood of reoccurrence of the severe misbehaviors. The risk factors are greatly increased when it is more likely that such behaviors will be repeated. It is important to not allow such activities to go on and on. It is recom-

mended that if the child has been placed on the program for oppositional behaviors the program be "temporarily" suspended to let any
danger pass but be reinstated after a professional therapist has been
consulted and had a chance to develop a working relationship with the
teenager. In other words, the therapist continues to work with the
child after the crisis is over while the program continues to operate.
Attention seeking, or secondary gains, may also underlie these behaviors. This is certainly a highly inappropriate way to get someone to
notice them, but nevertheless, it is quite common. Again, as stated in
the section on punishment, that by yelling and screaming at them the
parent may inadvertently be giving the child the attention they are
seeking and therefore be reinforcing these behaviors. Therapeutic intervention is indeed called for, but the program under these conditions
should also be suspended. The child may be gesturing in a way that is
asking for help. Give them that help with a professional. Again, after
the crisis is over resume the program. Attention seeking may occur
because the parents have been negligent. In which case family therapy
may be called for. Restructuring the child's attitudes about attention
and approval may be the direction therapy takes. The child may also
seek attention inappropriately because they lack the social skills necessary to get people to respond to them. In this case the therapist may
work directly with the teen to improve social skills. No matter what
cause underlies the attention seeking behaviors, the program goes back
into effect while the therapist works directly with the teenager. The
therapist should temporarily suspend the program only to stabilize the
child and decrease the danger level, but as soon as possible the program should be started again.
  Drugs and alcohol often underlie acting out behaviors. Chemicals
cause all types of inappropriate behaviors. As stated previously, the
youngster must be taken off the drugs immediately. When drugs and
acting out occur the danger level is probably high enough to merit immediate hospitalization. Impulse control is so markedly impaired that
the danger of harm to themselves or others is extreme. In a hospital
setting, if necessary, withdrawal procedures can be put in effect and
therapy begun. After release and while the child is in outpatient therapy the Tough Love program can be implemented. As stated previously, with the chemically dependent teen, money should not be placed in
their hands and therefore, it is not recommended to institute the REST
program.
  Depression, loneliness, feelings of worthlessness, and helplessness
may be underlying factors leading to the heightened acting out of suicide, running away, and delinquency. However, each of these is a

symptom and for a therapist to deal with them the causes must be fully and carefully assessed. Reactions such as these may possibly be signs of mental illness, but actually the majority of cases can be attributed to a set of precipitating problems in life that can be readily dealt with. Mental illness means there is something wrong with the person's brain chemistry, and even then under such conditions medications to treat such disorders are available. Problems in living means the disorders are precipitated by stresses in life and these too can be handled with the help of a therapist. Stress related disorders are presented in a typical therapist's office in far greater numbers. The majority of cases with teens are not the product of mental illness but more a result of the teen acting inappropriately to the stresses and pressures of life. Treatment for stress disorders does not mean your child is sick or mentally disturbed, but it does mean that he or she needs help in solving problems more effectively and getting their life back on track. In either case, these life problems do not excuse oppositional and abusive behavior. That kind of behavior is just not healthy and if anything they only serve to exacerbate emotional problems. The various REST programs are behavioral tools that are quite useful to get such discordant behaviors under control as quickly as possible. In the meantime, the therapist and the adolescent can work together to overcome any emotional or situational problems. The program is designed to complement the therapy by stabilizing the home environment and minimizing any home disruptions.

The therapist must entertain the possibility that when acting out occurs this may be a sign of abusive parents. Under such conditions the program itself can serve as a further abuse of parental power and certainly should be abandoned. The entire family would certainly appear to be in need of therapy. No one can be happy under such circumstances and the parents are urged to seek help with a professional just as soon as possible.

Parents should recognize that abuse to a child does not necessarily have to be physical or sexual; mental abuse can be equally and sometimes even more devastating to a child's emotional development. Neglect is another form of abuse which does not even have to be to the extremes of not providing food, clothing, and shelter but can simply be the result of being too busy for your child. It can occur when the parents are so busy that they fail to take an active interest in the child's activities, school work, and accomplishments.

Abuse can also come from overzealous parents who in desperately wanting their child to succeed in a difficult work inadvertently shout a litany of the child's shortcomings. Instead of praise in this environment there is constant criticism. The parents and the therapist must do an honest and objective appraisal of the quality of the parental interactions with the child.

Life crises can precipitate powerful emotional and behavioral responses in an adolescent. The death of a parent, illness, or an announcement of impending divorce can send the youth into a whirlwind of emotional turmoil. Depression and anger may exist and can be expected as normal reactions to such painful events. There are also behavioral manifestations that may appear at this time in the form of disruptions in the home and extreme acting out. If the child has not acted out previously but then suddenly following a major life event the misbehaviors begin, then the REST program should not be used to get the unruly behavior under control. Instead, the child would most likely be in desperate need for help with their grief. They need love and support and they need to express their emotions in the safe confines of a therapist's office. Only if oppositional behavior has been a long standing pattern beginning way before any crisis should the REST program be implemented.

It may be useful for the parents to have some familiarity with the observable symptoms of a clinical depression. When these symptoms are present in an adolescent it should serve as a red flag or warning sign to the parents to seek professional help. Severe depression is an emotional problem that can disrupt the normal body functions and behaviors. Look for the following ten basic warning signs:

1. Insomnia and Loss of Sleep
   The adolescent has trouble falling asleep and may be waking up several times during the night.
2. Low Energy and Chronic Fatigue
   The loss of sleep and the draining effect of the depression itself can immobilize the youngster's body.
3. Impaired Concentration
   So consuming is the depression that the child finds it difficult to mentally focus on anything.
4. Isolation
   The youngster has a strong need to be left alone most all the time.
5. Loss of Appetite and Weight Loss
   Most adolescents are eating machines. When you notice they are not eating, not even junk foods, and their clothing is becoming loose, this can be a warning sign.

6. **Frequent Crying**
   Even if they refuse to cry in front of you, this is most likely occurring if you frequently see their eyes reddened and puffy.
7. **Anxiety**
   They appear nervous, their face looks tense, and their eyebrows are furrowed with a worried look.
8. **Loss of Interest**
   Things they typically enjoyed such as the stereo, hobbies or sports no longer interest them. They just seem to want to lie around all of the time.
9. **Pessimistic Attitude**
   The youth verbalizes about depressing or bleak things. They are angry and bitter towards people and society. The past and the future are dark and bleak. They even feel badly about themselves. They may talk more about their inadequacies.
10. **Decreased Productivity**
    Grades suddenly drop. Their room becomes unkempt. Projects do not get finished.

Suicidal ideations are also frequently present. The risk of suicide increases when symptoms of depression are present. This may indicate the threat of suicide is not a manipulative gesture but a genuine desire to escape whatever pains the adolescent is experiencing. Furthermore, the teen may not see any solutions or ways the problem will ever come to an end. This can be a severe risk sign. Do not wait for a suicide note to appear before getting help since only one in four suicidal persons leave notes.

Whether a threat of suicide is believed to be genuine or merely a manipulative threat does not matter - get professional help! If your doctor recommends hospitalization, then cooperate. Suicide is one of the few acting out behaviors where the risks exceed the benefits of the program. Therefore, if suicide is even a remote possibility then suspend the REST program, at least until a professional has a chance to get the problem under control.

Runaway reactions and delinquent behaviors can also be frightening. However, the theme of accountability should persist when the behaviors occur. As a matter of fact, take a Tough Love stance. Let them know you will call the police and you will not bail them out. You will let them experience the consequences of their acts by allowing the law to do whatever is necessary. No high priced lawyer will be provided to protect them from irresponsible and rash behavior. These

71

behaviors must stop. Protecting them increases the likelihood of reoccurrences and therefore the risks of getting into severe trouble in another town or getting into a severe confrontation with a law officer. Nip it in the bud. Let the law scare them.

Many parents are concerned that having a record will destroy the youth's future. Doubtful, but it is a possibility. However, parents will soon discover that the more they protect their teenager the more likely reoccurrences will be and the more likely they will get a police record anyway. It is important to understand that these guidelines are not intended to apply to the youth that is a one-time offender or even a two-time offender. In other words these are drastic measures and should not be implemented until it is clear that these behaviors are not just a one-time tirade but the beginnings of a pattern. However, once it is clear that such behaviors will continue then the parent must learn to step aside and let the child learn from experience. They must experience the true consequences of such severe acting out. The rules of the home outlined in the program remain in effect. No matter how many times they run or commit a crime in an attempt to get you to terminate the program it is important to remain firm.

Considerably more can be said about extreme acting out behaviors and the reader is encouraged to obtain materials that are more exclusively devoted to these topics. This text's primary purpose is to focus on controlling oppositional behaviors through the REST program. If the oppositional behaviors escalate to the severe levels mentioned in this chapter then follow the specific guidelines given. Don't get discouraged.

Chapter 9

Special Problems

Divorce

There is plenty written on the topic of children's and adolescents' reactions to divorce. Certainly a youngster's grief and depression following a divorce need to be taken quite seriously and handled with great care and delicacy. Professional counseling may indeed be necessary. However, at the risk of being redundant, oppositional behavior is our current focus.

Oppositional behaviors often occur when parents are divorcing. In fact, one of the most frequent circumstances that arises in a divorce is the one where the parent who has custody reports to the ex-spouse that one (or more) of the children has become increasingly difficult to manage. It may be that the child has been oppositional long before the divorce but because of the divorce itself, the oppositional patterns may become even more apparent. It is also possible that after the divorce has been finalized the child may become oppositional as part of the anger that follows in the grieving process. Here the child may be expressing their anger toward their parents or may be lashing out because of the shocking disruption to their lives. However, it is my belief that the most frequent cause for oppositional behavior occurs when the child has assessed the power situations and has concluded that one parent alone, usually the mother, is not strong enough, physically and emotionally, to control them. They believe they can behave any way they want and there is not a damn thing the parent can do about it.

The custodial parent typically complains to the ex-spouse about these problems and frequently the complaints are met with incredulous disbelief. This often serves as a major source of dissension between both parties. I have seen this problem arise repeatedly. There are many possible reasons for its occurrence. The ex-spouse no longer witnesses the daily misbehaviors of the child and when the child pays a visit to them they do not display the same behavioral patterns. Often the child actually acts manipulatively and pours on the charm to get financial favors from a guilt ridden absent parent. Furthermore, the non-custodial parent is usually a male. Therefore, they are more overwhelming physically and the child unconsciously calculates the power setting and determines they darn well better be on their best behavior, or else.

Analysis of this circumstance can become even more complicated. It is not unusual for the child to switch behaviors with considerable skill. Divorce can precipitate insecurity in a youngster. In a desire for reassurance they may butter up one parent. Often this is directed toward the absent parent where the child has a heightened sense of insecurity. By being nice they elicit more praise and more expressions of love.

In addition to all this, the behavior of the parents can exacerbate the situation. There is often considerable amounts of anger between the ex-spouses. They will use any means to get even with each other. The result will be a prolonged period of cold warfare. It is not unusual to unwittingly use the children as weapons. One spouse may do everything to get the children to love them more than the other parent. For example, the ex-spouse may deliberately give the bare minimum of child support funds so that the necessities for living for the custodial spouse are scarce and luxuries are especially out of the question. When the kids come to visit the absent parent they are then showered with gifts of all types. Such manipulations are highly destructive to the emotional welfare of the children, but sadly are often of little concern to the parent when the war with their ex comes first.

One or both parents may say bad things to the children about each other. This is a frequent occurrence. It only serves to tear children apart emotionally. Often this is done to win a youngster over as an ally in the war against the other parent. The child typically gets caught up in these interactions and is encouraged to play the role of spy. By reporting bad things to one parent about the other parent they get a close and highly interested ear. This is both reassuring and reinforcing to the child but unfortunately such interactions create a very paranoid and emotionally unhealthy environment for a youngster to grow up in.

Further complications arise when one parent may deliberately be more lenient. When the children visit they can do as they please. The unspoken message sent to the children is, "See how mean the other parent is, because 'they' make you tow the mark! They're strict and I'm such fun."

It is not unusual under such a setting for the child to become disruptive and oppositional in the home of the custodial parent. Implementing the REST program becomes extremely important. It provides the custodial parent with substantial power to get the youngster under control. It is not healthy to allow the child to grow up in an atmosphere of manipulation and hostility. The REST program clarifies expectations and stabilizes relationships. However, it is common for the non-custodial parent to disbelieve the need for the program or even to sabotage the program. This is easily done by slipping the child lots of money. The program ends up being completely neutralized, and the youngster continues to be confused and disruptive. No one wins.

The main theme of this section is for divorced parents to realize what you are doing to your children. I hope you can begin to understand how your battles with each other are so completely empty. It is the children who wind up the victims when their emotional development is impaired by the childish antics of their parents.

The REST program is intended as a constructive tool designed to establish healthy and reasonable limits on a teenager's behavior. The teen will be happiest in a structured home environment where arguing is rare and where there is more time for love and caring.

Can the angry parent step back for a moment and realize what their attitude is doing to their children? Can such a parent realize that if they cannot get their feelings under control it is they that desperately need professional counseling?

Occasionally a frustrated parent will say to me that the ex-spouse thinks the program is silly. In each case I have found that the other parent is not familiar with the particulars of the program. Often they do not want good sense and logic to interfere with their holy war against the other parent. If you are concerned about your ex-spouse's treatment of you and the children at least try to get them to read this chapter of the book.

Surprisingly, many youngsters like the program. It gives them more money to spend and allows them more freedom in their choices of consumer items. However, most of all they seem to like the peace and stability that ensues. If both households enforce the program then stability will quickly follow and along with it a much happier and more content youngster.

Chapter 10

Communications

While the REST program is an effective tool for controlling the teenager's behavior, ultimately this is not what this book is truly all about. Controlling the teen is only a means to an end. The ultimate goal is a close and loving relationship.

When there is constant arguing and fighting not much of a relationship can develop. The mere elimination of the strife still does not mean a relationship has developed. It is communication that is essential if parent and child are to become close. Parents often interpret this to mean that it is the child that must learn to communicate. Actually, if this program is to succeed then the parent must also learn effective communication skills.

I will outline steps toward effective communication shortly. Before starting, however, I must strongly state that whatever procedures are given for communication they are meaningless in the absence of love. I am well aware that almost every parent loves their children, but as they become teenagers there is a tendency to say it less and less. As the teenager begins to demonstrate obnoxious testing behaviors we may become angry and then the displays of love diminish even more. For communications to succeed, we absolutely "must" tell the adolescent we love them and we must show them our love. It is important to hug and kiss and show our deepest affections. Do not assume that they automatically know you love them; it must be said and shown.

The REST program eliminates disharmony in order to help rekindle an atmosphere for love and affection. In this way the door to communication is open. The following steps are suggested to foster better communications.

Step 1 - Judgment

Judgment is a rather vague term to which many specific definitions can be applied. Judgment means choosing when and where a communication should take place to enhance contact with each other. When something needs to be said parent and teenager will probably want to be alone in a quiet place.

Judgment also means selecting intelligently what you wish to communicate about. Forcing a teenager to talk about and discuss everything is not a good rule for effective communication. Select wisely. When negative things occur then choose those topics and problems that are of uppermost concern to you. Attempts at overcommunicating about negative things diminish its effectiveness.

We usually think of communicating only when problems arise. This means we reach out for each other from crisis to crisis. We therefore only talk to each other when we are filled with negative feelings. This should be far from the only contacts we have. Communication should also be a time of sharing positive and constructive thoughts and feelings. We, as parents, can accomplish an awful lot of teaching if we patiently share our views, motives, problem solving techniques, beliefs, and values about many, many things. It is in this way that we develop intimacy with our young and encourage them to learn about life from us. Remember in the early part of the book we talked about separating Life and Home issues. I stated then that arguing blocks effective communications about Life. The program is not even half completed if we are merely controlling behaviors in the Home. The major work in parenting is to set the stage for closeness and communicating. I remember an old television show called The Courtship of Eddie's Father where father and son walked quietly side by side discussing many things and dad patiently tried answering his son's questions about life. I truly suspect that if parents would do this sort of thing regularly with their children, starting very early in life, the closeness between parent and child that would evolve would nullify the necessity of ever even needing the REST program in the teenage years. When there is such closeness then a mere look of disapproval or disappointment would be devastating to a youngster and serve as a strong motivator to modify their behavior. Of course to develop this closeness necessitates the parent spending time with their teen. The time should be positive - quality time. For example, for many years my oldest daughter and I have taken a few hours, and even an entire day, away from the rest of the family. We've gone fishing, canoeing, tubing, walking, picnicking, exploring theme parks, hiking, and on and on. During these times we get to know each other. We talk about anything either of us feels like. Not only does she slowly learn about my feelings, thoughts, and values over many issues but I learn about her attitudes about things. In this way I truly believe we have grown close. I must say that these days are great for me because by the end of the day I feel marvelously at peace and content. Try it with your children individually. I think you will be surprised at how delightful these moments are in both you and your child's lives.

Step 2 - Initiation

Initiation means taking the responsibility of expressing what is on your mind, when necessary, and in as positive a way as possible. The basic method of initiating comes under the huge topic of Assertion. There are many wonderful books available on Assertion and the reader is encouraged to read several. A suggested bibliography appears in the index of this book. The topic is too extensive to be fully covered in this text.

The ideas behind assertiveness involve three aspects. First, is non-assertiveness. Non-assertiveness means holding something in and not saying anything about what is bothering you. This usually leads to a storing of bad feelings with the ultimate consequence of both of you continuing to suffer needlessly until one of you reaches a dangerous exploding point. Do not assert over every little issue but for major problems make an early effort to take care of business. The second aspect is Aggressiveness. In psychology, aggressive behavior is defined much more broadly than in layman's terms. It not only means physical aggression, yelling, and screaming, but it also means addressing someone in a harsh and clipped manner. It means badgering mercilessly and being insensitive to your impact on the other person. It means cornering them and not letting up. It means lecturing, lecturing, lecturing. It means the subtleties of a kind of body language and tone of voice that create an atmosphere of tension. Such aggressive communication techniques are ultimately quite injurious to the parent-teenager relationship. The teenager either keeps quiet non-assertively, and builds a powerful resentment toward you, or he lashes back abusively and angrily. Furthermore, when we are Aggressive we are modeling those very behaviors we do not like in our teenagers. Do not forget modeling is the most powerful method of teaching. We must be honest with ourselves and objectively assess how we behave to our children. If we are ever going to teach them responsible behavior then we must behave responsibly. Then we can demand that our teenagers not behave aggressively toward us. We must "require" them to eliminate "all" aspects of aggressive behaviors, including the more subtle patterns of sarcasm, and tongue in cheek forms of disrespect. The third aspect is

79

learning assertive methods of communication. This means requiring that they must learn to think objectively and clearly and then to express these thoughts effectively. Learning to be assertive means learning how to talk so that other people will willingly want to listen to what you have to say. It is a delicate balance between teaching them to speak up when something is bothering them and their having a big mouth. Patiently and painstakingly take the time to teach children what assertive communications are all about, and then set the limits as to the way you will be addressed. They will learn that if they wish to communicate with you it can be accomplished calmly and with respect.

I truly believe it is one of the most difficult tasks for two people to calmly sit down, face each other, and cooperatively work through a problem. It is far easier to say nothing or to explode in anger posturing and gesturing in an intimidating manner. When I ask parents to learn assertive communication techniques I am well aware I am asking them to take on one of the most difficult tasks they have ever faced. Not only is it important to learn the verbal behaviors of assertion but equally important to learn the skills of thinking assertively. Most difficulties in assertion begin with faulty thinking. Without our being aware of it we frequently misinterpret reality. Thought precedes behavior. We frequently think thoughts that work us unnecessarily into a frenzy. We often think in an overreactive, catastrophic, and demanding way. When this happens our feelings increase way out of proportion to the situation, and in turn the behaviors that result are way in excess of the situation. Instead of constantly solving the problem what does all this accomplish. It alienates the other person involved, it upsets us, and it does not solve the problem. When we learn to think rationally, we soon discover that very few circumstances are of monumental importance. We begin to realize that peace and serenity can be of our own creation. It is important to learn to stubbornly refuse to get upset over every trivial thing and to structure our thoughts, feelings, and behaviors to be in harmony with serenity. When we learn to think assertively we will learn that assertive communication follows readily.

Step 3 - Reception

If one person is talking the other must be listening, otherwise there is no communication. Probably a skill even more difficult to learn than assertion is Active Listening.

I must credit my wife and daughter for patiently teaching me the true meaning of active listening. As a therapist, when working with patients I practiced active listening with great diligence. Unfortunately, I let my brain relax in my private life and found I allowed myself to miss a lot. My wife taught me the true meaning of better communications by modeling excellent listening skills with our little girl. She would point out to me what my daughter was trying to say. Gradually I began to realize that my daughter had a wonderful and active mind and I needed to more readily grasp the insights and ideas she was trying to convey. I realized how important it was not to be so mentally lazy with the people I love.

Active listening means paying attention, interpreting, evaluating, and exerting energy into understanding what the other person is saying. Strife in families would decrease enormously if everyone would do these things. I have found in adolescent counseling, and even in marriage counseling, that differences are far less than people perceive if only they would take the time to truly listen to what the other person is saying.

If you wish your youngster to discontinue abusive verbal behaviors and to learn assertive habits then you must learn the skills of active listening. They must learn that they can get your attention without resorting to such antics. In turn, if your adolescent wishes for you to stop the lecturing and the badgering then they must develop these same skills. Improved communication will not just happen unless both of you learn and practice better listening habits.

If you wish true communication to occur with your teenager then you'd best be prepared to hear things you probably do not want to hear. If you are going to discuss Life issues with them then you will hear things about sex, drugs, career, friends, etc. that may astonish you. By keeping the lines of communication open you can at least know more of what is going on in their lives and exert some influence over moderating their activities. Your reactions will determine whether or not they continue to communicate and turn to you for advice or whether they go underground and shut you out completely. For simplicity's sake, I can group inappropriate reacting patterns into three categories: (1) overreacting, (2) underreacting, and (3) no reacting.

Overreacting involves an exaggerated pattern of heightened behavior. This could come in the form of yelling, screaming and pounding the table. You do not like what you heard so you hit the ceiling. Your thoughts precede your reaction, and when you overreact you can bet that your thoughts are of catastrophic overproportions. You interpret what you heard as terrible, awful, "I can't stand it", it should not and must not be - but indeed it is, and overreacting typically not only does not help matters in the slightest but only serves to cut off communication. Underreacting, the second inappropriate pattern involves acting hurt, injured, and depressed by what you hear. The underlying cognitions involve self pity, and exaggerating matters as a personal issue. Typically the thought, and the resulting reacting is in excess to the reality of the situation. No reacting means saying nothing, and staring blankly. It means not coming back with a response. It is a rather common complaint that occurs when there are communication problems. No one can have any idea what is going on inside a person who shows no response, and this can be very frustrating to a teenager that has just shared something very important with you.

All this does not mean do not react. It simply means not to react in an exaggerated, disproportionate way. Think rationally and behave realistically. In this way you and your teenager can continue a dialogue and work this and future problems through.

Step 4 - Debate

Initiation and reception are only the beginning of communication. An exchange must ensue. A meaningful exchange of ideas, thoughts, beliefs, feelings, attitudes, and reactions are important components for clearing the air.

This step, to be productive, must be done calmly, directly, and honestly. This is a difficult task for a teenager and parent to do.

There are several things people do to prevent this step from being productive. First, parent and/or teenager often drift off the topic. They begin discussing extraneous and irrelevant things. To be productive in communication people must learn to stick to the topic. When you realize you have strayed off the topic remind the other party and return to the issue at hand. You will spend a lot of time going nowhere if you constantly permit yourselves to drift. The second problem involves having multiple items that you wish to discuss. Nothing is accomplished by dealing with them all at one time. Issues get muddled and confused when they are not covered separately and singularly. Again, stick to one topic at a time. Do not try to cover too much territory all at once. If one issue takes particularly long you and your teenager can schedule additional time for continuing the discussion and gradually finishing all the things you want to cover. Third, the parent and teenager use the debate not to discuss a problem but instead to throw cross accusations at each other. This continues going nowhere. Reserve these other accusations, if they are important, as additional items to be discussed later. Fourth, the debate step can easily turn into a yelling match. When one party begins to feel overwhelmed or incensed by something said there is a tendency to want to subdue the other person with raw aggressive power. You may in fact get them to shut up but you have not won them over to your ideas.

Remember that communication does not merely mean talk, talk, talk. It means discussing the most sensitive, most explosive, most embarrassing, and most emotionally ladened things. It is important to work at keeping your thoughts and your emotions in check throughout the entire process. Finally, debate does not mean nagging. Nagging is a frequently used strategy designed to wear your opponent down. In fact, one of you may win a particular point but in the long run neither of you has learned to effectively communicate. Then additional future problems will only end in the same frustrating way. This step is perhaps the easiest one to get off track and it is often the one where teenager and parent get bogged down.

Step 5 - Solutions

Once you have expressed all your thoughts and feelings it is important to proceed even further. The issue was brought up in the first place because one of you wanted something done about it. A communication is not resolved until a constructive answer is found.

Many people appear to have difficulty getting past the debate stage. It seems that arguing and stubbornly refusing to see the other person's point of view are more important than resolution. Often we are not listening carefully to all the arguments presented. Oddly, I have found that as a neutral party, when I listen to each person's point of view it is obvious that very frequently they are not all that far apart.

For a solution to be found both the parent and the teenager should weigh very carefully whether their attitude is conciliatory or whether it is downright stubborn. Indeed, there are certain issues where taking a firm stand is important. However, the vast majority of issues are far less important than the destruction each episode of combat between teenager and parent is causing in their relationship. If we realize that "the relationship comes first," then the secondary importance of all the issues that come up are put into proper perspective. When you remember this rule you will realize most issues are compared to the closeness and integrity of the family unit.

Often parent and teenager are overwhelmed emotionally in trying to iron out a difference of opinion. A useful technique that I have taught over the years may help break a stalemate. Simply make a written list of all the possibilities for solutions both of you can think of. You are not stuck with any particular solution at this point. You are merely listing them. Free associating all the possible solutions you can think of without censoring anything is a technique called brainstorming. List the solutions in order, from the solution where the parent gets 100% his way, to the solutions where the teenager gets 100% his way, and include all the possibilities in between. Often when the list is complete a solution will become apparent that both of you can feel comfortable with. If this does not happen, then each of you ask how far away you are willing to move. When both of you choose a newer, more conciliatory position you will probably notice you are only one or two steps apart. When both of you reach that point, it often becomes apparent that if you give in just a little more you can arrive at a peaceful and livable solution.

Step 6 - Honor

One or both of you may wind up feeling short changed by the solution agreed upon. It then becomes easy to have a hidden solution agenda to sabotage things. This is a dirty deeds technique called passive-aggression. On the surface the parent acts as though they were interested and caring of the teenager's point of view. All along they knew if the end product did not turn out their way they would then deliberately and secretly mess things up. I not only view this as unethical conduct but an excellent way to teach your teenager to be underhanded.

When a solution is arrived at it is important for both of you to honor it. Do everything you can to make it work. If the situation truly appears untenable rather than passive-aggressing, communicate your feelings of deep dissatisfaction and request a return to the drawing board. Generate new ideas and come up with a new solution. You will not get your teenager to voluntarily cooperate with you if he soon discovers that you are going to do things your way anyway and that you are unscrupulous in how you will go about getting what you want.

There can be no true communications without honor.

Chapter 11

A Case Study

Kim's parents, as instructed, appeared for the initial intake appointment without her. They were a handsome couple neatly dressed in casual clothing. Both people were warm and personable. They conveyed an air of genuine and deep concern for their fifteen year old daughter.

Both parents took turns talking, expressing anger, frustration, worry, and disgust. The years of tension were very apparent. Kim was nearing her sixteenth birthday and the problems had been progressively worsening for over three years, beginning in the eighth grade, just before she turned thirteen. The parents painted a fairly typical profile of an oppositional teenager. They stated at the outset that they had been to two other therapists, once for three months and once for six months, but no changes occurred. They discontinued therapy each time because they felt they were not being given specific answers and there was no evidence of progress.

At home when Kim spoke to her parents it was usually in a sarcastic tone. Often, it appeared as if she could barely stand to stay in the same room with them. This behavior was not only almost a daily occurrence but often would actually persist throughout an entire day. When she was required to listen her eyes would roll and her mouth took an impatient turn downward. If something was said that she did not like she would shoot chilling hate stares. Kim also had a rather volatile temper. One or two times each week she would explode over something rather trivial, such as her twelve year old sister using her hair dryer. When she would have a temper tantrum she would yell as loud as she could at whoever's turn it was to be her target. Profanity was a frequent part of her repertoire. On at least five occasions during the previous year her parents reported that Kim used physical violence such as pulling her sister's hair, hitting her mother across the face, and throwing glass objects, smashing them against a wall. Her parents claimed they never used physical punishment and could not recall ever spanking Kim.

Parental reports further seemed to indicate that Kim went out of her way to taunt her twelve year old sister. She frequently criticized her sister about her appearance, choice of clothes, her good school grades, and her relationship with her parents. They argued almost daily. The parents were concerned because the younger sister, Barb, was beginning to demonstrate the same early patterns of belligerence as Kim. They were frightened and wanted the process stopped immediately.

Other adults in the immediate neighborhood praised Kim to her parents as being such a "wonderful child" and an excellent role model, wishing all their kids would be just like her. Oddly, this is not unusual since many teenagers pride themselves in their abilities to manipulate adults. As part of this manipulation their behavioral pattern is selective. When she is with other adults she readily turns on the charm, but with her parents, she behaves monstrously. Kim's friends were mostly high school sorority sisters. The parents report that almost all of them were very pretty and seemed to take great pains to dress extremely well in rather expensive clothing. However, Kim's parents had a very strong feeling that, just like Kim, almost none of these youngsters were to be trusted. Several of the other parents have reported similar problematic behaviors as Kim's occurring in the privacy of their homes. As with many teenagers, Kim seemed to place primary importance on her peer relationships. She preferred being with her friends almost daily. The parents were fairly secure that drugs were not a major issue. Kim had said many times that she strongly felt drug taking was stupid. She had consistently looked well physically, with no evidence of lethargy, dilated-watery eyes, impaired speech, sleep problems, or appetite problems. It seemed that the main source of bonding for this peer group had been an overzealous obsession with boys. Kim's parents felt certain that she had had sexual relations, but there was no absolute proof. On three occasions in the past year they checked Kim's room in the middle of the night only to discover that she had snuck out. They suspected that since her room is on the second floor she climbed down the drain pipe outside her window. Each time Kim returned home at about five o'clock in the morning at which time an argument with her parents followed. Kim would stick to her story that she could not sleep and just went for a walk. The parents stated that they felt certain Kim lied frequently about many things but often there was not any way to prove otherwise.

In the evening hours Kim withdrew to her room. She apparently judiciously avoided socializing with the family. Either she blasted the stereo or she stayed on the telephone. She talked on the phone every evening and conversations at times have lasted well past midnight. The parents took the phone out of the room for weeks at a time only to return it when she pleaded and promised that she would stop her abuse of the phone. The improvements would last perhaps one or two weeks and then she returned to her typical patterns. Family friends complained of constantly getting a busy signal when trying to call. The parents asked this therapist what my thoughts were about their getting Kim her own private phone. I suggested that we would discuss the issue after we set about changing Kim's behaviors.

School performance had been a major source of concern for Kim's parents. Her grades in elementary school were mostly A's and B's. Her final report card at the end of the eighth grade consisted of "C's" and "D's". Subsequent report cards had been similar with an occasional "F". Teachers reported that there had been no problems with conduct. She usually avoided talking to teachers and when attempts were made at engaging her in conversation outside the classroom she would answer quickly and politely and then say something about having to leave. In class she seemed disinterested. Teachers described her as frequently doodling or tapping her pen as if she could not wait for class to be over. They indicated that her attention span was typically short. Voluntary participation in class discussions had been rare and when called upon without raising her hand teachers had stated that it was not unusual for her to be unaware of what was being discussed. Homework had been either not done, incompletely done or messy. She had been known to copy homework from her friends. Teachers occasionally referred her to a school counselor but she did not appear for her appointments. Overall she conveyed an "I don't care" attitude. Her last report card included the following grades:

Math (Algebra)	D
English	C
Science (Biology)	D
World History	F
Art	B

She attended summer school the previous year to make up grade deficiencies and successfully passed everything. This year it appeared that she would have to attend again.

Kim's personal hygiene and appearance were judged by her parents to be excellent, but they claimed her room was a disaster area. Clothes were rarely hung and could be found draped over chairs or lying on the floor. This necessitated very high cleaning bills. Her bed was never made. Her mother occasionally found moldy food, such as old pizza or hamburger, under Kim's bed. The only time the room was clean was when her mother became fed up and did it herself. Kim left the upstairs bathroom in a shambles. She participated in none of the housework. Barb had also begun demonstrating the same patterns in this area.

After the initial intake interview with her parents Kim appeared for her first appointment one week later. She was a very pretty young lady. She seemed quiet and somewhat shy. Her voice was so soft that several times I asked her to speak more loudly. Attempts at small talk were designed to make her comfortable. However, she developed a response style of answering as briefly as possible and frequently shrugging her shoulders and stating "I don't know," "I guess," or just smiling and snickering politely. She was very skilled at passive-aggressively avoiding any substantive dialogue. This pattern was to continue throughout the course of involvement with this case. Repeated invitations over time were made to engage in talk therapy but her attitude appeared fairly fixed. Such a pattern is quite typical with oppositional teenagers and attempts at repeated weekly appointments considering the type of dialogue I truly believe are a waste of the parents' time and money.

An intelligence test was administered and indicated that Kim was fairly bright. Her I.Q. was about 124 which indicates that with most modest effort she is capable of A and B grades.

Therapeutic intervention was initiated with two instructional sessions with the parents. They were given lessons on the REST program. Target behaviors included:

- oppositionalism, including: eye rolls, hate stares, sarcastic tone of
  voice, talking back, yelling, and refusal to talk
- cursing
- lying, including sneaking out
- physical aggression
- overuse of the telephone
- sibling fights, mostly instigated by Kim
- messy room
- not participating in household chores
- poor school performance
- isolating herself from the family
- not honoring curfew hours

Level I rules and consequences were to be begun immediately after an evening was set aside to fully explain the program and its purposes to

Kim. As expected Kim did not like the entire thing and summarily told her parents, including me to "Go to Hell!" In addition to Level I collateral programs were initiated for Lying and Aggressive acting out, and for School Performance. A new private telephone line was being installed for Kim's phone which would henceforth only remain in operation if she maintained the monthly payment from her allowance. She was forbidden to use any other phones. If she were caught using another phone this would be construed as deceipt and an item would be lost from the Lying program list.

The following were Kim's rules on the Level I Program:

Rule 1 - Hygiene

> Kim was to be neatly dressed and ready for school Monday through Friday by exactly 7:00 a.m. Her room was to be straightened each day, and the bed made before leaving for school.

Rule 2 - Chores

> The following major chore list was to be followed.

Major Chores:

> Monday - To do all her own laundry and ironing.
> Tuesday - Vacuum entire house.
> Wednesday - Dust furniture throughout entire house.
> Thursday - Cook family dinner.
> Friday - Clean all bathrooms (4) thoroughly.
> Saturday - Thoroughly clean her own room, including
>   closet straightened, vacuum entire room,
>   change linens, dust, desk and dresser
>   straightened, etc.
> Sunday - Assist her mother, father, and sister in
>   general housecleaning.

Minor Chores:

> Daily - clean bathroom after using; pick up and fold or hang personal clothing; pick up and put in kitchen sink all dirty dishes and glasses she uses; assist with

cleaning kitchen and dining room after dinner.

Rule 3 - Verbal and Physical Abuse

Talk and act appropriately to parents and sister. The following will
not be allowed:

1. Yelling at parents and sister
2. Cursing
3. Physical violence - touching anyone, breaking or throwing
   anything
4. Eye rolls and hate stares
5. Sarcastic comments
6. Snide comments
7. Refusal to respond

Disagreements and differences are to be discussed calmly.

Rule 4 - Safety

Curfew:
Sunday through Thursday - 5:30 p.m. home in time for family
                                    dinner
Friday and Saturday - 1:00 a.m.

Tell parents exactly where you are going to be. Any changes or
problems, call home.

Collateral Programs:

Program I - Lying and Aggression

The following list are objects to be removed for one year if Kim is
"suspected" of lying, including sneaking out, or if Kim acts violently
by either touching someone or breaking something.

1. Dating
2. Driver's license
3. Personal telephone
4. Personal room stereo
5. Personal television
6. Portable stereo

Program 2

Each Friday Kim is to have her teachers fill out a grade report sheet and bring it home to be reviewed by her parents. Any single grade below a "C" or any performance below an "S" will result in the loss of that weekend's privileges - Friday night to Monday morning. Forgeries or misrepresentation lead to loss of item listed on lying list and Kim is grounded that weekend.

Kim was given full instructions in the operating of the program, she was also told about the higher Level programs that would be implemented if Level I failed, and what she was told would happen to her if she ran away. The program was begun.

As expected, Kim refused to cooperate. As a matter of fact, matters got worse. She was more belligerent than ever. Parents should be aware that the worsening of behaviors after initiating the program is a common occurrence and that they should not be discouraged. This condition is usually a temporary attempt by the teenager to have the program terminated. Apparently, she was determined to be as sloppy around the house as she could. The parents clearly saw that if Kim persisted she would be pulling the financial noose tighter and tighter and that conditions would only get worse for her. Finally, after week four, Kim showed a drastic turnaround. She said nothing but simply began to comply. However, that week she only earned her allowance one day. Apparently she was testing the waters by breaking at least one rule every day. Each evening she received an envelope with a note carefully explaining why no allowance was given. She was not allowed out on weekends for failing to bring home the grade report sheet. She lost items six and five for violent outbursts. Even though Kim was trying it would have been a major mistake for the parents to give in at the first signs of improvement and give Kim her allowance without meeting "all" the criteria. Giving in would only reaffirm Kim's attitude about continuing to test her parents' patterns or inconsistency and of them always giving in. This only encourages a continuation of Kim's testing behaviors. Finally, she began to comply more diligently. During week six she earned her allowance four out of seven days, which of course without the bonus was not even close to meeting her financial needs.

The phone company called inquiring about her missed payment. Kim assured them she would send a check immediately. Shortly afterward insufficient funds led to her phone being disconnected. It was her responsibility to pay for and reestablish the connection. This ultimately took several more weeks.

91

Week eight of the program was the first time Kim met the bonus requirements. She had complied with all the rules for seven days. Her parents actively reinforced her socially. All seemed well. On a Wednesday night of the following week she disappeared. The police were called. Kim and a boyfriend had driven to a horse barn about fifteen miles outside of town. They were found asleep in the morning by the owners who had called the police. Both youngsters were taken into custody. Kim's parents refused to come to court to sign her out of detention. A caseworker had seen her parents where the program was explained to him. The caseworker seemed to like it and agreed to cooperate. Within a few days Kim appeared before the judge who had the police return her home. She was warned by the judge of stronger consequences if it happened again. It never did.

Once again Kim refused to comply with the program. Notes on the evenings and weekend groundings continued until the twelfth week. Finally, Kim began to comply with all aspects of the program. Her parents reported a dramatic change in her attitude, as if she were grateful for the newly imposed structure on her life. She was invited to visit with me which she accepted. Her parents said she was anxious to talk with me but when she did appear she continued her monosyllabic response patterns.

Kim's parents reported the following improvements:

Hygiene - 85% improvement
Chores - 90% improvement
Verbal and Physical Abuse - 90% improvement
Safety - 100% improvement

Lying and Aggressive patterns stopped completely. School grades improved to about a "C" level. However, her teachers reported a dramatic improvement in participation and attitude. Her parents and teachers said she seemed like a much happier child.

Therapy began to focus on the parents for several months. During the interviews with Kim it was discovered that she knew that her mother went through her things and read her mail. It was pointed out to the parents how this violated Kim's right to privacy and in addition they could not, and should not, expect Kim to stop lying and being deceitful if they insisted in such subterfuge. The mother hid behind the excuse of being worried about Kim getting into drugs. The inconsistency and dishonesty of this statement was dealt with. That is, previous sessions indicated that the parents truly were not that concerned over drugs. Kim's mother had to work on her tendencies to be over-controlling and overbearing. The mother slowly began to realize that there may indeed be some substance to Kim's withdrawal from her. Such behavior does not elicit respect from a teenager and is not conducive to ever developing a positive relationship founded in trust. After a few sessions the mother began to see the point. The concepts of separating the limits of parental responsibility were once again carefully reviewed. Further sessions dealt with the mother's overall attitude of control and her methods of manipulating the members of the family. While she rarely raised her voice and generally tended to remain polite she constantly maneuvered the family into doing whatever she believed was best for everyone. She employed dishonest methods such as saying "Well, if it's what you want, O.K." and then proceeding to do things exactly her way. Overall the mother was quite skilled at what are termed passive-aggressive behaviors. Her behaviors were pervasive with all members of the family and even how she dealt with outside friends. The mother viewed herself as a scrupulously honest and forthright person. It took quite some time before she began to realize that not only was she dishonest in the way she communicated and behaved with her family, but that her behavior patterns actually modeled the lying she found so offensive in Kim. While the mother began to comprehend, this therapist felt she would have difficulty in giving up such well established habits and attitudes. I tried to impress upon her the importance of honesty and directness in the overall emotional wellness of the family. However, she really was not interested in therapy for herself, all she wanted was Kim straightened out. Further therapy was recommended for her but unfortunately, she declined.

Kim's father had equal difficulty dealing with some of his problems. Actually, when working with teenagers I have found it is frequently a thorny problem to get the parents to examine their own behaviors and attitudes and to make personal changes. I have found it is relatively easier to not only get the teenagers to change but to teach them how to cope with parents who stubbornly refuse to change. Parents often bring their teenagers to a therapist with the mental set of "fix my kid", and "I'm not here for me." Such attitudes make the work of the therapist quite difficult. Kim's father proved to be a relatively good patient. Once confronted, he admitted some of the changes on which he needed to work and he was quite cooperative. He loved Kim and for her sake he seemed ready to help. His most pronounced problem was his temper. On occasion, he would blow up and with clenched fists he would strike hysterically at inanimate objects. He often pounded on the car dashboard and cursed when the car was slow to start. Again, such behaviors serve as a model for a teenager to follow.

Kim's father made some dramatic changes after he understood their importance.

Consistency appeared to be a problem both parents had to work on. Giving in too easily with Kim, inconsistently applying rules, and inconsistently enforcing consequences were detrimental to Kim's improvement. These patterns only encourage a teenager to test conditions. Instead of being forced to learn new habits the teen only goes through surface motions of change, covertly they believe they can wait things out and eventually the old system will be back in effect and once again they can have their way. Kim's parents had to learn the rule that inconsistency teaches persistency.

With Kim and Barb well under control and with some parental changes having been made, the family elected to terminate therapy. They were quite happy with the results. Thus after five months, therapy was terminated.

Approximately seven months later Kim's mother called frantically requesting an appointment. She indicated that everything fell apart and Kim was just as impossible as ever.

When they came to the office it was apparent that indeed Kim's behaviors had relapsed considerably. The parents confessed they had gradually become lazy and increasingly were inconsistent with the program. They often forgot to give Kim her allowance. They resorted to the old patterns of badgering and yelling.

When Kim came in she seemed glad to see me. She was not any more happy with conditions at home than her parents. She was looking to me to straighten out the mess. She said the program brought peace to the family for the first time in years. As a matter of fact, it was she that asked to see me. She was angry and frustrated at not getting her allowance when she had been trying so hard, and finally she felt there was no use. Her parents' badgering and lecturing was getting on her nerves. She was especially angry that her mother was still reading her mail and going through her belongings. She stated that she could not stand her mother. Her mother's self-righteous attitude over the family was a constant souce of annoyance.

The parents confirmed what Kim had said. I pointed out that the program works when used consistently, but that it was not a substitute for changing attitudes. I stated that I would go no further with this case unless Kim's mother entered therapy. It was the failure of the parents to make meaningful changes in their attitudes about consistency, responsibility, and honesty that led to the collapse of this program. The parents agreed to do whatever was necessary.

This time Kim's mother appeared much more interested in cooperating in personal changes. She worked on more assertive and direct methods of communicating and gradually she abandoned her indirect, passive patterns. She also learned to accept Kim's responsibilities and she relinquished her desire to overcontrol Kim's life.

Kim initially made only moderate improvement. While her parents were more consistent Kim was only earning her allowance three or four days each week. This level of improvement was insufficient. After two months of this pattern the parents were given instructions to issue the one warning indicating that if improvement was not imminent then Level II would be started. Kim had learned to be more persistent because of her parents' inconsistency and now it was she that would be paying the price. After two weeks Kim did not improve and Level II had to be started. Kim's behavior immediately got worse. The parents were frightened and disillusioned. Four weekends of grounding went by without Kim meeting the criteria of six days of earning her allowance to earn her weekend privileges. Finally, Kim had begun to comply, and success was achieved.

I saw the family once a month after the situation was back under control. Level II stayed in effect one full year with only periodic occasions when Kim did not meet criterion. After a year we returned to Level I. Things went smoothly. After several weeks Kim and her parents made a request to try functioning without the program. I was very pleased because this said to me that everyone sensed dramatic changes in Kim's attitude and felt safe to give it a try. It was recommended that Kim be given her allowance non-contingently, that is it would not be tagged onto the rules, and that she follow the rules voluntarily. The money would still be used, as before, to purchase items she judged she needed. This was agreed to and I am pleased to report that events went smoothly.

The overall course of treatment was far from smooth. Rarely does psychological treatment with teens follow a smooth course. I strongly urge parents when beginning the REST program to keep in the forefront of their minds that improvement will indeed be a rough road. It is not realistic to expect that by merely instituting the program everything will be perfect. At all cost, remain on track and stay consistent. When the teenager begins to fight and test the program deprivations for the things they want and enjoy will automatically increase dramatically, and eventually they will comply. Hang in there through thick and thin. Be patient.

A few years later, just before Christmas, I was in my office one afternoon catching up on paperwork when I received a call from Kim's father. In a broken, tearful voice he thanked me for the best possible

Christmas present. Kim was in college studying to be a teacher and he stated that they had grown close. Kim was now a responsible and apparently happy young adult. I felt wonderful - what a beautiful Christmas present that was for me.

Chapter 12

Not the Final Chapter

I began the development of the REST program several years ago, mostly out of frustration. In working with teenagers I kept trying to apply a hodgepodge of various psychological techniques. I increasingly felt inadequate. I began realizing that in all my years of training and practice nothing had adequately prepared me to deal with difficult teenagers. My training focused on understanding the teenager's needs, wants, fears, anxieties, and developments, but nothing seemed to help control them when they were out of control. I went to a major university library and diligently reviewed the literature. I found nothing. With the help of the librarian a computer search was done - nothing! Actually, I was astonished. It was difficult for me to believe that there was such a void in psychological treatment. Gradually, the ideas of the system presented in this book developed. I tested and refined the ideas case after case and I was pleased to discover that the system worked. However, I truly believe this is only the beginning. It is my fondest wish that newer techniques and improved methods be developed. In essence, once a new idea is crystallized it seems to set the stage for a surge of insight and understanding for further advances. I certainly hope we are now on our way. This book is written for parents and for professional therapists. With their cooperative efforts and insights perhaps some unhappy teenagers will benefit.

One of my major concerns is observing how confused parents are these days. It seems that parents over the last twenty or more years have been intimidated by psychology, psychiatry, and education into believeing that it is bad, detrimental, and psychologically scarring to be firm with their chidlren. Parents have become afraid to require almost anything of their children such as help with housework, talking respectfully, dressing appropriately, being courteous, etc., etc. Parents feel guilty if they deprive them of anything, and so they feel the pressure to flood the young with a wealth of material goods. The result has been youngsters made into helpless victims who are unable to sustain effort for longterm meaningful goals. By cushioning life, parents have distorted the youngster's development of tolerance for stress. We have trained the young to NOT THINK. Then, after the parents have supplied their children with an abundance of comforts they are flabbergasted when the thanks they get is disrespect and obnoxious and insensitive behavior. The usual reaction of the parent to this is emotional, and often includes lots of arguing, yelling and screaming. We have been so thoroughly indoctrinated in understanding the teenager that we have forgotten the need to control them. It is our responsibility to train them in appropriate conduct and behavior.

This is not an invitation for parents to become abusive, and powerful authoritarian figures. It is an invitation to love our children in a responsible way. This means we must give them tons of tender and sensitive love. We must understand their wants and needs. We must learn how to communicate with them, and this includes hearing what they have to say. However, this also means we must know what limits to set on them and how to accomplish their behaving appropriately within these limits.

Any scientific tool can be used to improve the conditions of society or it can be used abusively to destroy the society. The techniques developed here are intended to improve the loving parent-child relationship. This tool can be used abusively. Parents are encouraged to exercise soundness of judgment. The techniques are intended to require respectfulness from our teenagers. If they are overused to dominate their every breath we actually defeat our purpose of healthy development and thereby block their abilities to think and problem solve.

When positive behavior and communication is achieved in the home the parent then must give the teen the freedom to allow them to experience life. We must lay back and let them experience the consequences of their actions and on their own to resolve conflicts and difficulties that come their way. If turmoil has been reduced in the home then in times of trouble the teenager will come to you for guidance.

Use the program wisely.

References Consulted

Adams, David B. (1980). Adolescent Residential Treatment: An alternative to institutionalization. Adolescence, XV, 59(Fal), 521-527.

Alexander, James F.; Barton, Cole; Schiaro, R. Steven and Parsons, Bruce V. (1976). Systems behavioral intervention with families of delinquents: Therapist characteristics, family behavior, and outcome. Journal of Consulting and Clinical Psychology, 1976 (Aug), 44(4), 656-664.

American Psychiatric Association: Diagnostic and Statistical Manual of Mental Disorders, Third Edition. Washington, DC:APA, 1980.

Anderson, Lowell; Fodor, Iris and Alpert, Murray. (1976). A comparison of methods for training self-control. Behavior Therapy, 7(5), 649-658.

Barkley, Russell A.; Hastings, James E.; Tousel, Robert E. and Tousel, Susan E. (1976). Evaluation of a token system for juvenile delinquents in a residential setting. Journal of Behavior Therapy & Experimental Psychiatry, 7(3), 227-230.

Bernal, M. E.; Klinnert, M. D.; and Schultz, L. A. (1980). Outcome evaluation of behavioral parent training and client-centered parent counseling for children with conduct problems. Journal of Applied Behavior Analysis, 13, 677-691.

Besalel, V. A. and Azrin, N. A. (1981). The reduction of parent-youth problems by reprocity counseling. Behavior Research & Therapy, 19(4), 297-301.

Braukmann, Curtis J.; Ramp, Kathryn Kirigin; Tigner, Drenda M.; and Wolf, Montrose M. (1979). The Teaching-Family approach to training Group-home parents: Training procedures, validation research, and outcome findings. In S. C. Feinstein and

P. L. Giovacchini (eds.), Adolescent Psychiatry, Developmental and Clinical Studies, VII, (pp. 144-161). Chicago, IL:The University of Chicago Press.

Burquest, Bret. (1979) Severe femal delinquency: When to involve the family in treatment. In S. C. Feinstein and P. L. Giovacchini (Eds.), Adolescent Psychiatry, Developmental and Clinical Studies, VII (pp. 516-523). Chicago, IL:The University of Chicago Press.

Carpenter, Patricia. (1984). "Green Stamp Therapy" revisited: The evolution of 12 years of behavior modification and psychoeducational techniques with young delinquent boys. Psychological Reports, 54(1), 99-111.

Chabot, David R. (1976). Family therapy with court-committed, institutionalized, acting-out, male adolescents. Clinical Psychologist, 29(4), 8-9.

Chassin, Laurie; Young, Richard D. & Light, Roger. (1980). Evaluations of treatment technique by delinquent and disturbed adolescents. Journal of Clinical Child Psychology, 9(3), 220-223.

Crabtree, Loren H. (1982). Hospitalized adolescents who act-out: A treatment approach. Psychiatry, 45(2), 147-158.

Dumas, Jean E. (1984). Interactional correlates of treatment outcome in behavioral parent training. Journal of Consulting and Clinical Psychology, 52(6), 946-954.

Elder, John P.; Edelstein, Barry A. & Narick, Marianne M. (1979). Adolescent psychiatric patients: Modifying aggressive behavior with social skills training. Behavior Modification, 3(2), 161-178.

Elitzur, Baruch. (1976). Program for acting-out adolescents. Adolescence, XI, 44, 569-572.

Everett, Craig A. (1976). Family assessment and intervention for early adolescent problems. Journal of Marriage & Family Counseling, 2(2), 155-165.

Eyberg, S. M. & Johnson, S. M. (1974). Multiple assessment of behavior modification with families: Effects of contingency contracting and order of treated problems. Journal of Consulting and Clinical Psychology, 49, 900-907.

Faretra, Gloria. (1981). A profile of aggression from adolescence to adulthood: An 18-yr. follow-up of psychiatrically disturbed and violent adolescents. American Journal of Orthopsychiatry, 51(3), 439-453.

Fehrenbach, Peter A. and Thelen, Mark H. (1982). Behavioral approaches to the treatment of aggressive disorders. Behavior Modification, 6(4), 465-597.

Fineberg, Beth L.; Sowards, Stephen K.; & Kettlewell, Paul W. (1980). Adolescent inpatient treatment: A literature review. Adolescence, 15(60), 913-925.

Franks, Cyril M. (1979/Sum 1981). Behavior therapy with children and adolescents. Annual Review of Behavior Therapy Theory & Practice, 8, 273-304.

Franks, Cyril M. (1982). Behavior therapy: An overview. Annual Review of Behavior Therapy Theory & Practice, 8, 1-38.

Gelman, David (1986, January). Treating teens in trouble: Can the psychiatric ward fill in for the family? Newsweek, 52-54.

Goldstein, Arnold P. et al. (1978). Training aggressive adolescents in prosocial behavior. Journal of Youth & Adolescence, 7(1), 73-92.

Goldstein, Arnold P. and Pentz, Mary A. (1984). Psychological skill training and the aggressive adolescent. School Psychology Review, 13(3), 311-323.

Grady, F. Patrick. (1983). Treating violent male adolescents in a therapeutic residential milieu. Milieu Therapy, 3(2), 53-61.

Gross, Alan M. and Brigham, Thomas A. (1980). Behavior modification and the treatment of juvenile delinquency: A review and proposal for future research. Corrective & Social

Psychiatry & Journal of Behavior Technology, Methods & Therapy, 26(3), 98-106.

Hall, James A. (1984). Empirically based treatment for parent-adolescent conflict. Social Casework, 65(8), 587-495.

Harbin, Henry T. (1977). Episodic dyscontrol and family dynamics. American Journal of Psychiatry, 134(10), 1113-1116.

Harbin, Henry T. and Madden, Denis J. (1983). Assaultive adolescents: Family decision-making parameters. Family Process, 22(1), 109-118.

Hobbs, Tom R. and Holt, Michael M. (1976). The effects of token reinforcement on the behavior of delinquents in cottage settings. Journal of Applied Behavioral Analysis, 9(2), 189-198.

Janzen, William B. and Love, William. (1977). Involving adolescents as active participants in their own treatment plans. Psychological Reports, 41(3, pt 1), 931-934.

Kagan, Richard Mark. (1983). Engaging family competence to prevent repetitive and lengthy institutionalization of acting-out youth. Residential Group Care & Treatment, 1(3), 55-70.

Kaufman, R. F. and O'Leary, K. D. (1972). Reward, cost, and self-evaluation procedures for disruptive adolescents in a psychiatric hospital school. Journal of Applied Behavior Analysis, 5, 293-309.

Kazdin, A. E. (1979). Advances in child behavior therapy: Applications and implications. American Psychologist, 34, 981-987.

Kellner, Jacob. (1975). A model for differential treatment of the juvenile delinquent. Mental Health & Society, 21(1-2), 55-65.

Kennedy, James; Mitchell, Janet B.; Klerman, Lorraine V. & Murray, Andrew. (1976). A day school approach to aggressive adolescents. Child Welfare, 55(10), 712-724.

Kirigin, Kathryn A.; Braukmann, Curtis J.; Atwater, Jay D.; & Wolf, Montrose M. (1982). An evaluation of Teaching-family (Achievement Place) Group homes for juvenile offenders.

Journal of Applied Behavioral Analysis, 15(1),. 1-16.

Lewis, Dorothy O. and Balla, David. (1975). "Sociopathy" and its synonyms: Inappropriate diagnosis in child psychiatry. *American Journal of Psychiatry*, 132(7), 720-722.

Lewis, Dorothy O.; Lewis, Melvin; Unger, Lisa & Goldman, Clifford. (1984). Conduct disorder and its synonyms: Diagnosis of dubious validity and usefullness. *American Journal of Psychiatry*, 141(4), 514-519.

Machalow, Rosalie. (1982). Psychiatrically hospitalized adolescents. *Adolescence*, XVII, 68, 789-799.

Madden, Denis J. and Harbin, Henry T. (1983). Family structures of assaultive adolescents. *Journal of Marital and Family Therapy*, 9(3), 311-316.

Maloney, Denis M.; Timbers, Gary D. & Maloney, Karen B. (1977). Bringing it all back home (BIABH) project: Regional adaptation of the teaching-family model group home for adolescents. *Child Welfare*, 56(1), 787-796.

Marohn, Richard C. (1979). A psychiatric overview of juvenile delinquency. In S. C. Feinstein and P. L. Giovacchini (Eds.), *Adolescent Psychiatry*, Developmental and Clinical Studies, VII, (pp. 425-432). Chicago:The University of Chicago Press.

McHolland, James D. (1985). Strategies for dealing with resistant adolescents. *Adolescence*, XX, 78(Sum), 349-368.

McMahon, R. J.; Forehand, R., & Griest, D. L. (1981). Effects of knowledge of social learning principles on enhancing treatment outcome and generalization in a parent training program. *Journal of Consulting and Clinical Psychology*, 49, 526-532.

McMahon, Robert J. and Forehand, Rex L. (1983). Consumer satisfaction in behavioral treatment of children: Types, issues, and recommendations. *Behavioral Therapy*, 14, 209-225.

Moreland, John R.; Schwebel, Andrew I.; Beck, Steven & Well, Robert. (1982). Parents as therapists: A review of the behavior therapy parent training literature - 1975-1981. Behavior Modification, 6(2), 250-276.

Moss, Gene R. and Rick, Gary R. (1981). Application of a token economy for adolescents in a private psychiatric hospital. Behavior Therapy, 12(4), 585-590.

Neapolitan, Jerry. (1981). Parental influences on aggressive behavior: A social learning approach. Adolescence, 16, 64(Win), 831-840.

Neff, Pauline. (1982). Tough Love: How parents can deal with drug abuse. Nashville, TN:Abingdon Press.

Ney, Philip and Mulvin, Deanna. (1982). Case report on parent abuse. Victomology, 7(1-4), 242-251.

Phillips, Debora. (1975). The family council: A segment of adolescent treatment. Journal of Behavior Therapy & Experimental Psychiatry, 6(4), 283-287.

Plapp, Jon M. (1983). Some characteristics of adolescents who present significant management problems in residential psychiatric treatment. Australian Psychologist, 18(1), 107-115.

Roberts, Randy. (1982). Treating conduct-disordered adolescents and young adults by working with the parents. Journal of Marital & Family Therapy, 8(3), 15-28.

Robinson, Paul A. (1978). Parents of "Beyond Control" adolescents. Adolescence, XIII, 49(Spr), 109-119.

Ross, Robert and McKay, H. Bryan. (1976). A study of institutional treatment programs. International Journal of Offender Therapy & Comparative Criminology, 20(2), 165-173.

Rossman, Paul G. and Knesper, David J. (1976). The early phase of hospital treatment for disruptive adolescents: The integration of behavioral and dynamic techniques. Journal of the American Academy of Child Psychiatry, 15(4), 693-708.

Ro-Trock, G. Kelton; Wellisch, David K. & Schoolar, Joseph C. (1977). A family therapy outcome study in an in-patient setting. American Journal of Orthopsychiatry, 47(3), 514-522.

Rueger, Drue Barrett and Liberman, Robert P. (1984). Behavioral family therapy for delinquent and substance abusing adolescents. Journal of Drug Issues, 14(2), 403-418.

Rutherford, Robert B. and Bower, Kenneth B. (1975). Behavioral contracting in cojoint family therapy. Family Therapy, 2(3), 215-226.

Schimel, John L. (1979). Adolescents and families: An overview. In S. C. Feinstein and P. L. Giovacchini (Eds.), Adolescent Psychiatry, Developmental and Clinical Studies, VII, (pp. 362-374). Chicago:The University of Chicago Press.

Schloss, Patrick J. (1983) An integrated social learning approach to the treatment of aggressive reactions. Education, 104(1), 104-112.

Schneiderman, Gerald and Evans, Harvey. (1975). An approach to families of acting-out adolescents: A case study. Adolescence, 10(40), 495-498.

Shamsie, S. Jalal. (1982). Antisocial adolescents: Our treatments do not work - where do we go from here? Annual Progress in Child Psychiatry & Child Development, 631-647.

Shapiro, Edward R. and Kolb, Jonathan E. (1979). Engaging the family of the hospitalized adolescent: The multiple family meeting. In S. C. Feinstein and P. L. Giovacchini (Eds.), Adolescent Psychiatry, Developmental and clinical studies, VII, (pp. 322-342). Chicago:The University of Chicago Press.

Shapiro, Roger L. (1979). Family dynamics and object-relations theory: An analytic, group-interpretive approach to family therapy. In S. C. Feinstein and P. L. Giovacchini (Eds.), Adolescent Psychiatry, Developmental and clinical studies, VII, (pp. 118-135). Chicago:The University of Chicago Press.

Sherman, Barbara. (1972). The adolescent in family therapy. Family Therapy, 1(1), 35-48.

Smith, Thomas E. (1983). Adolescent reactions to attempted parental control and influence techniques. Journal of Marriage & the Family, 45(3), 533-542.

Sonis, Meyer. (1979). Aichorn revisited: A report on acting-out adolescent behavior. In S. C. Feinstein and P. L. Giovacchini (Eds.), Adolescent Psychiatry, Developmental and clinical studies, VII, (pp. 484-495). Chicago:The University of Chiago Press.

Stumphauzer, Jerome S. (1976). Modifying delinquent behavior: Beginnings and current practices. Adolescence, 11(41), 13-28.

Tramontana, Michael G. (1981). Critical review of research on psychotherapy outcome with adolescents: 1967-77. Annual Progress in Child Psychiatry & Child Development, 521-550.

Wagner, Bernard R. and Breitmeyer, Rudolf G. (1975). PACE: A residential community oriented behavior modification program for adolescents. Adolescence, 10(38), 277-286.

Weathers, Lawrence and Liberman, Robert P. (1975). The family contracting exercise. Journal of Behavior Therapy & Experimental Psychiatry, 6(3), 208-214.

Weathers, Lawrence; Liberman, Robert Paul. (1975). Contingency contracting with families of delinquent adolescents. Behavior Therapy, 6(3,, 356-366.

Welch, Gary J. (1976). A procedure to augment contingency contracting. Journal of Behavior Therapy & Experimental Psychiatry, 7(3), 301-303.

Wilson, Rich. (1984). A review of self-control treatments for aggressive behavior. Behavior Disorders, 9(2), 131-140.

York, Phyllis and David and Wachtel, Ted (1982). Toughlove. New York:Doubleday and Company, Inc.

About the Author

David B. Stein is currently Assistant Professor of Psychology at Longwood College, a Virginia state-assisted college. He completed his doctorate in Clinical Psychology in 1978 at Virginia Commonwealth University. He has served as a staff psychologist in mental health centers and in an acute care psychiatric hospital and was director of psychology services at an adolescent home in Tennessee. From 1979 to 1985, he owned and directed a private psychology clinic while practicing as a clinician and serving as Clinical Assistant Professor at the University of Tennessee Center for the Health Sciences. He has lectured and written on a broad range of topics but feels his central focus at present involves his research and writings on adolescence.

Made in the USA
Coppell, TX
24 June 2021